P9-DVJ-234

3 1404 00818 8929

JUN 15 2007

Computers Thinking and Learning

Inspiring students with technology

David Nettelbeck

ACER Press

WITHDRAWN

MAY 0 7 2024

DAVID O. McKAY LIBRARY
BYU-IDAHO

First published 2005
by ACER Press
Australian Council for Educational Research Ltd
19 Prospect Hill Road, Camberwell, Victoria, 3124

Copyright © David Nettelbeck 2005

All rights reserved. Except under the conditions described in the *Copyright Act 1968* of
Australia and subsequent amendments, no part of this publication may be reproduced,
stored in a retrieval system or transmitted in any form or by any means, electronic,
mechanical, photocopying, recording or otherwise, without the written permission of the
publishers.

While every effort has been made to check the currency of web sites, the publisher does not
accept responsibility for the content of web sites referred to in this publication. Likewise,
reference in the publication to web sites or products does not constitute endorsement of
them, and no financial benefit has been received by the author or publisher from products
and services referred to.

Edited by Margaret Trudgeon
Cover and text design by Polar Design
Printed by BPA Print Group

National Library of Australia Cataloguing-in-Publication data:

Nettelbeck, David Clive.
   Computers, thinking and learning: inspiring students with technology.

   Bibliography.
   Includes index.
   ISBN 0 86431 779 4.

   1. Computers – Study and teaching (Secondary). 2. Electronic data processing – Study
   and teaching (Secondary). 3. Information technology – Study and teaching (Secondary).
   4. Thought and thinking – Study and teaching (Secondary). 5. Learning – Study and
   teaching (Secondary). I. Title.

   004

Visit our web site: http://www.acerpress.com.au

Inspiration® is a registered trademark of Inspiration Software®, Inc.
ProBoards® is a registered trademark of Patrick Clinger. All rights reserved.
SchoolKiT™ and EDclass™ are registered trademarks of SchoolKiT International.
All rights reserved.
CorelDRAW® is a registered trademark of the Corel Corporation. All rights reserved.
Microsoft® and PowerPoint® are registered trademarks of the Microsoft Corporation.
All rights reserved.

Foreword

I first came across David Nettelbeck's work when I was undertaking, with a group of colleagues in the UK and New Zealand, a review of research on the relationship between literature teaching and information and communication technology (ICT). David's was one of the few pieces of research that got to the heart of the link between research, policy and practice on this topic, and it did so with integrity, verve and validity. Then I met him and heard him speak about the topic at the 2003 International Federation of Teachers of English conference in Melbourne. My initial impression was confirmed: that this was someone whose practice and reflection were cutting edge, and someone whom teachers, researchers and policy-makers ought to follow – just as his students probably do!

It is therefore an honour to be asked to write a foreword for *Computers, Thinking and Learning*. My own thinking about the relationship between new literacies and computers has moved on from the 2003 conference, much inspired by people there and by further reading in the field. In 2003, and in some writing before and after the conference, I wondered whether we needed to resurrect Christine Haas' notion that the relationship between literacy/literacies and ICT was symbiotic rather than causal and one-way. In other words, the conventional point of view was that most researchers seemed to assume that computers had come along

and influenced reading, writing, viewing, speaking and listening in various ways. They did not, on the whole, consider that, in turn, patterns and types of communication might have a backwash effect on interface design and computer use itself. They did not recognise that technologies and literacies develop alongside each other.

Whereas Haas enables us to move beyond the one-way vision of the effect or impact of ICT on literacy and literacies, I now think that symbiosis is not the most accurate way to describe what is going on. After discussion with biologists at the University of York, UK, my hunch is that we need a model to describe and explain the relationship between computers and literacies that sees it as *reciprocal co-evolution*. Symbiosis suggests a conservative relationship: one in which the two parties sustain each other and want to keep it that way. Reciprocal co-evolution is a more accurate descriptor because it accepts that the two parties are continuing to develop.

Such a dialogic vision of the way computers and literacies interact is entirely in concert with this book, in which David explores the potential and actualities of thinking and learning in the classroom. The book accepts and promotes the idea that ICT is no monolithic entity, but rather a range of different technologies, media and modes of communication (the biologists will be asking me next to write a phylogeny or genealogy of types of ICT). Furthermore, the book also accepts that literacy is no longer conceivable as a monolithic set of practices, but instead has to be seen as a number of different literacies or sets of social, communicative practice (another phylogeny). How these two phylogenies map onto each other and can inspire teachers and students to explore new ways of expression and communication is the subject of this book.

In practice, the transformations that this book has in mind are of the kind that English and humanities teachers have been practising for a long time: the taking of a text or utterance and transforming it in the classroom into something else. For example, the reading of a short story can generate the writing by students of a letter from one character to another, or the creation of some spoken and acted role-play. With the added dimension of ICT, the range and nature of those pedagogic transformations are multiplied. Learning and thinking in such a classroom has the potential to be colourful, varied and highly motivating. Some of the key strategic decisions that teachers and students have to make are: what is the best format for what I want to say? Why am I using ICT in this particular context? What forms of hybrid text are possible? What am I going to learn by undertaking particular transformations? Which are the richer and more challenging transformations in terms of getting me to think and in terms of communication with particular audiences?

Answers to these and other questions will be best made if we consider what Richard Lanham calls 'the economics of attention'. The question of what we do with our and our students' consciousness in the precious hours that are devoted to language and literary studies in the school curriculum is ever more important in a world where the demands on consciousness and the channels of communication are increasing. From the point of view of an economics of attention, learning in which transformations take place will be a good use of time in that they will have a social life in the classroom (and perhaps beyond) and also a transformative effect on internal thinking and reflection.

This book offers many approaches to such transformations, and it places ICT and computers in a wider economy of forms and means of communication which can be drawn upon as appropriate (or inappropriately, for fun and subversive purposes). We have moved beyond the first phase of the use of computers in classrooms where futurologists were predicting (again) the end of the book and of literacy and learning as we knew it. Now that computers are taking their place in the repertoire, we can see more clearly their advantages and disadvantages for particular occasions of communication. The particular structure of this book, in which classroom applications are set within learning contexts, and in which further suggestions are offered for teachers to follow up in their own ways, is ideal for busy teachers who need a guide that is authoritative, up-to-date, imaginative and inspirational. David Nettelbeck's work and this book are exactly that.

Richard Andrews
University of York

Contents

Preface

Computers, Thinking and Learning is about thinking and learning in the digital age and how computers can be used to enrich these processes. 'The old computing was about what computers could do; the new computing is about what users can do. Successful technologies are those that are in harmony with users' needs. They must support relationships and activities that enrich the users' experiences.'[1]

Teaching has been a long and changing roller-coaster journey for me. When I began, the technology consisted of blue wax stencil sheets, pen, radio, tape recorder and chalk. Whether I like it or not, I now teach in a world of laptops, the Internet, online resources, electronic submission of work and a whole new concept of what the terms 'reading' and 'literacy' mean for the cyber-kids, the N-Generation, the 'screen-agers' or whatever euphemism we may devise for our current students. For many of them, the traditional classroom is almost becoming an alien world. Today's teachers have no choice but to re-conceptualise what the terms literacy and literacy education actually mean.

The ideas in this book have been distilled from classroom experiences over many years, but particularly during the last decade when I have been privileged to work with amazingly open and supportive groupings of colleagues. Many of the examples in this book have been drawn from the English classroom because that is the scene I know best, but the skills and applications are often generic and could be applied across a wide range of subjects.

In the early days of computers in schools I was one of a largely self-selected group of interested teachers who met for breakfast every few weeks to share ideas and encourage each other in what were essentially pioneering and risk-taking teaching practices. After several years of some exciting forward thinking, genuine collegial support and great professional stimulus, this rather esoteric 'think tank' group was disbanded. I owe an enormous debt of gratitude to that 'breakfast club' and also to some fine professionals in several schools who have been prepared to exchange ideas and take risks. Throughout the book I have tried to acknowledge the help of specific colleagues, but it can be hard to recollect and pinpoint the exact source of good ideas when these are often mulled and discussed over coffee or on the run between classes. To all those I have worked with, I offer my sincere thanks.

The best ideas get nowhere unless they can be applied, and our most critical audience is always the students. Some of them found it tedious being the guinea pigs, as they saw it, and would occasionally ask with a sigh, 'Are you experimenting on us again?' Most, however, found classes with laptops or computers in labs refreshingly different and were not afraid to reflect on the changing nature of their learning. I have included examples of many students' work, mostly unedited and from across a range of abilities and year levels. In every case, the students have willingly given me permission to show other teachers their work and a few have said, 'I would be so proud for someone else to see what we have been doing'. It has been impossible to acknowledge every individual student contribution but I am grateful to all those whose work is reflected here and all who have taught me so much.

I have also been privileged to conduct workshops for teachers from more than 100 schools across five states in the last few years. Teachers attending workshops have come from a range of schools and systems, and from middle primary to upper secondary. The workshops have never been just a one-way skills transmission exercise but a genuine interaction between many fine professionals. I have, in fact, never conducted a session without acquiring something myself to try out in my own classes. I learnt in my early teacher training days that the best teachers are also the best parasites. I trust that the experiences I have been able to garner from so many colleagues may be a catalyst to the thinking and practice of those who read this book and that you too will unashamedly borrow ideas, modify them and, in turn, pass them on.

David Carter believes that the introduction of information and communication technology into classrooms over the last ten years 'has led to some of the most creative thinking about the way we teach and learn in schools'.[2] In an ideal world, or one that is hopefully coming to every classroom soon, students will access computers or laptops on a one-to-one basis. The computer will then become a very rich resource within a genuinely personal workspace. 'It just doesn't work to schedule time for children to go to the computer lab. The information and communication technologies (ICTs) need to be a material part of the learning environment.'[3]

Some of the best work I have seen with laptops has been in government schools where students choose to purchase a personal computer and 80 per cent of the classes at a year level work with laptops. However, there are other good models. In one school, students are required to have a computer at home where they do online retrieval of tasks for homework from the school's network and upload their submissions. It limits flexibility of classroom teaching but is a good compromise. In another school there was abundant lab access to computers with restrictions on the IT classes so that their demands did not become the 'camel in the tent' and take over the labs. I have also seen banks of computers in the back of secondary classrooms with encouragement for teachers to use group work and flexible learning programs, much like we so often see in primary schools.

We do not need sophisticated commercial programs or elaborate front-end organisers for our intranets, helpful as these might be. You will find that most suggestions in this book are simple and achievable in Word, with a few in PowerPoint. I have also found Inspiration and SchoolKiT extremely useful and I recommend these commercial software packages (with an assurance that I gain no financial advantage from doing so).[4]

What we all need, rather than glitz and glamour, is strong and visionary educational leadership, supportive colleagues, helpful technical assistance and a climate that encourages simple risk-taking.

Just start in a small way and have a go.

Please do not hesitate to e-mail me if you would like an electronic copy of any of my own text material in this book or if I can help in other ways. The email address is davidnettelbeck@bigpond.com, or write to me via ACER Press, Melbourne, Australia.

David Nettelbeck

Endnotes

[1] B. Schneiderman, *Leonardo's laptop: human needs and the new computing technologies*, MIT Press, Cambridge Massachusetts, 2003, p. 2.

[2] D. Carter, 'The role of teachers in the school of the future'. Abridged from a paper presented at the Technology Colleges Trust's Vision 2020 Online Conference 2002, *Snapshots: The Specialist Schools Trust Journal of Innovation in Education*, Vol. 1, No. 1, July 2003.

[3] S. Holden, 'Just connecting', *Professional Educator*, Vol. 3, No. 3, September 2004. Report of an interview with Di Fleming, former school principal and now Associate Professor of Digital Design at RMIT University, Melbourne, Australia.

[4] See Appendix 2 for further details.

In memory of our son
Peter
1976 – 2004

who challenged the ordinary

and without whose encouragement this book may never have been completed.

Author's Acknowledgements

I am grateful to many whose support and willingness to break new ground with me have kept me optimistic. I am especially grateful to:

my ever patient wife Rosalie and my supportive, extended family;

Tony Hewison and Fr Paul Cahill, who gave me the rope to run with;

the editors of ACER Press, who glimpsed some potential in early journal articles I had written and helped me hone my ideas and experiences into this current shape;

Bruce Dixon and Jenny Little, whose workshops, conferences and support have given me a strong desire to explore the many ways in which new technologies can enrich and transform the teaching and learning environment;

many, many colleagues whose willing exchange of classroom experiences have stimulated my own thinking. My particular thanks to Di McDonald for her generosity in sharing her ever-flowing creative ideas and who fulfilled so admirably the role of a critical friend;

Professor Richard Andrews for his valuable research, perceptive insights and very generous Foreword.

Source Acknowledgements

p. 15 'Caught Reading' by Mike Lane, The Baltimore Sun. © Copyright 2004 Mike Lane; p. 32 From: *This Side of Silence, Poems 1987–1990*, Bruce Dawe, Pearson Education (Longman), 1990; p. 33 'Only Nineteen' words and music by John Schumann © Universal Music Publishing. All rights reserved. International copyright secured. Printed with permission; pp. 35–6 'Small-town dream', reproduced with the permission of Kathielyn Job; pp. 35–6 Annotations by Year 9 students Kerry Matthews and James Waters; p. 37 'Bury Me' by Chu Hsiang. Translated by Kai-Yu Hsu. Published in Richardson, P., Watson, K., & Gill, M (eds) 1998, *Snapshots of Planet Earth: An anthology of international poetry*, Oxford University Press; p. 37 Annotations by Year 9 student Kerry Matthews; p. 38 'Smugglers' © Maria Lewitt. Published in O'Connor, M (ed.) 1988, *Two Centuries of Australian Poetry*, Oxford University Press. Reproduced with permission of Maria Lewitt; p. 39 Poem extract from: *This Side of Silence, Poems 1987–1990*, Bruce Dawe, Pearson Education (Longman), 1990; p. 39 'Rusting Junkyard' photo © 2004 Amanda Pinches; pp. 41–2 'The Ivory Trail' © Victor Kelleher, 1999. Published by Penguin Books Australia, 1999; p. 47 Reproduced by permission of Mehdi Sadeghi, Cartoonists & Writers Syndicate / cartoonweb.com; p. 53 'Grandmother's Hands' photo © 2004 Anne Peterson; p. 60 main image © 2004 Amanda Pinches; inset image © Digital Vision; p. 60 'Afternoon Tea' photo © 2004 Amanda Pinches; p. 84 Table prepared by Year 11 student David DeAngelis. He gathered the sound files from http://www.frogs.org.au, the web site of the Amphibian Research Centre which has links to the Victoria Frog Group; p. 94 Reproduced by permission of A. Moir, *The Sydney Morning Herald*; p. 95 Reproduced by permission of John Spooner, *The Age*; p. 97 Reproduced by permission of John Cole, *The (Durham, NC) Herald-Sun*; p. 98 *The Shawshank Redemption*; Director: Frank Darabont; Producers: Liz Glotzer (executive), David V. Lester (executive), and Niki Marvin; p. 104 Cartoon strip © 2004 Robert D'Alberto; p. 105 Extract from 'But you didn't' by Merril Glass, published in *Latitude: Exploring and creating poetry*. Edited by Lisa McNeice, Oxford University Press, 2002; p. 105 'Formal dress' © 2004 Scott Cheslin; p. 119 Lesson reproduced with permission of SchoolKiT International; p. 120 Left slide – photo © 2004 Anne Peterson; p. 142 Extract from *The Lost Salt Gift of Blood* by Alistair McLeod published by Jonathon Cape. Used by permission of The Random House Group Limited; p. 149 'Boat' and 'Train' images and text copyright © 2004 Will Allen; p. 149 'German Soldier' PowerPoint slide text © 2004 James Magree; p. 149 'Annabelle' PowerPoint slides © 2004 Tom Yore. Photo of gaunt woman © 2004 Amanda Pinches. Every effort has been made to acknowledge and contact copyright owners. However, should any infringement have occurred, ACER tenders its apology and invites copyright owners to contact ACER.

Chapter 1

'However noble, sophisticated or enlightened proposals for change and improvement might be, they come to nothing if teachers don't adopt them in their own classrooms and if they don't translate them into effective classroom practice.'[1]

Management initiatives:
Who leads the renaissance in your school?

The learning and thinking context

Perhaps we are asking the wrong questions if we want to know what computers can do for us. Ben Schneiderman sums this up by reminding us that 'Computing today is about what computers can do; the new computing will be about what people can do'.[2] Ask yourself where your school or faculty stands when looking at the following table.

The old computing	The new computing
Focus on what computers can do. Teachers get excited about the 'aha' moment when something new and exciting works.	Focus on what people can do with computers, not on what computers can do for people.
Technician and technology driven. Focus on bits and bytes, connectivity. Teachers often told to adapt their classroom practices to fit the system.	Driven by the curriculum and learning goals of the forward thinking educational leader in the school. User-centred not technology-centred.
Better ways of • marketing the school • presentation • vocational preparation • research • communication • re-drafting • organising/storing	Better ways of • using multiple intelligences • analytical thinking • visual analysis • facilitating • collaborating • empowering • discovering • making and doing
Generally teacher-controlled, didactic learning.	Potential for open-ended, pupil-centred, constructivist learning.

Management initiatives:
Who leads the renaissance
in your school?

Computers provide us with a whole new way of thinking about teaching and learning; they are the vanguard of a communications revolution that is changing society, and in particular schooling, as much as the printing press did 600 years ago. Glimmers of this are beginning to appear as the risk-takers and innovators, who are also experienced teachers, work with like-minded and supportive colleagues to question some of the paradigms upon which classroom practice has previously been built. 'There is no question that ICT leads to changes in classroom organisation which places new demands on teachers and successful integration of ICT depends on teachers managing these demands.'[3] Information, Communication and Technology (ICT) can be a powerful motivator for learning when used wisely, while research is showing that it can also be a powerful de-motivator if the educational goals are not clear, there is poor network connectivity, or the initiatives are not sustained.[4]

Classroom strategies

Let us be quick to take account of the ubiquitous influence of technology in the world of our students. We hear them say things such as: 'I like to do things my way', 'Give me the information, skills and tools and let me get on with it', 'visuals appeal to me more than text', 'I can take responsibility for my own learning process', 'I believe that breadth of experience is as important as depth', 'I need to be involved, to do it myself'.

If we are to fulfil the potential of this new learning paradigm, there are three key areas that teachers need to concentrate on:
- personal organisation and planning;
- classroom management and expectations; and
- factors quite beyond the control of the teacher.

Personal organisation and planning

Let me begin with a personal anecdote. I began teaching with laptops as an add-on to classroom management practices that I had long been used to, including some blackboard work, some discussion, some reading of the text and some student response in each 50 or 60 minute lesson. Laptops appeared to cause immense frustration. The network would go down so online resources could not be accessed; log-on time could be affected by network connectivity issues or more commonly by music or games files that were using up computer memory; some students would forget or lose their blue cords or wireless cards to connect to the network; others just wanted a few minutes to send their homework for another subject or access e-mail because the school was expecting students to read notices but rarely gave them an opportunity in the timetabled day to check vital information about things such as sport or music rehearsals. There were a plethora of other excuses, and the student who was reluctant to have pen and paper ready was just as reluctant to maintain a laptop in good working order.

I also found myself very frustrated at my inability to get the students' heads out of the screen when I wanted them to listen to me or engage in group discussion, pay attention to oral presentations or share literature together. I still see computer-mediated communication as one of the positive gifts to this generation, but I also fervently believe in face-to-face relationships where facial expressions and body language are vital elements in building trust and understanding. The occasional teachable 'aha!' moment in a poetry or drama lesson, when faces light up, is rare enough, but even more rare if students are tempted to keep their eyes glued to the computer screen.

In order to minimise these problems in a one-to-one laptop or desktop classroom (where every student has access to a computer), I tried designating certain lessons in which students could bring and use their laptops, and other lessons when they were firmly told to leave them in their lockers. In these latter lessons we went together to the library for fiction reading, or listened to poetry, shared the class novel, discussed the current media topics in groups or listened to oral presentations from peers. Brabazon calls such face-to-face teaching a 'tactile, aural, visual, sensory explosion of possibilities',[5] and these are vital moments for any teacher.

In exchange for this computer ban in some periods, I set modules of one or two weeks' duration which could be completed in some designated class-time and for homework and in any order. Students could therefore choose whether to read in class and do Web research at home, discuss a creative writing task with a group and work on it together, or work alone on a poetry response. This gave enormous flexibility and choice, and a far greater sense of control of their learning for those willing to take the rope and run with it.

To my surprise, many were able to reflect, with some insight, into the enhanced quality of their learning experiences. Of course, others who did not generally do pencil and paper homework were not enthusiastic about this kind of work either, and for some, I had to build in intermediate checkpoints through the week to ensure that they did not sink into a mire of despair on the date when the whole module was due. It was also a great spur to me to ensure that I planned lessons well in advance and a check that I included some elements of poetry, writing, fiction and oral in each module. The amount of face-to-face teaching actually increased and I was able to allow more time to help those who needed it, while others were glad to be left alone, immersed in their various self-chosen tasks.

It is advisable to have computer-

Management initiatives:
Who leads the renaissance
in your school?

free days when students don't access their e-mail and the network. David Lyon, Professor of Sociology at Queens University, Kingston, Canada, says,

> We must rest from gathering information just as the ancient Israelites rested from gathering food at least one day a week. Likewise … we should regularly practice media fasts: days or weeks during which we reduce the flood of information to the merest trickle … We say we are frustrated by having so much to respond to, but we still carry cell-phones everywhere and check our e-mail every ten minutes. It makes us feel important to be so busy. Media fasts should help us to become more honest about our motivations.[6]

Perhaps we need to be more honest also about real engaged learning and meaningful classroom interactions.

One of the more significant achievements to come from the way of working outlined above was that I was able to get away from the curse of the worksheet culture, where there are narrowly defined lists of tasks. When these kinds of tasks are set the good students often race through them and think that they have learnt something while the weak students use their well-developed avoidance strategies and think they are clever to have beaten the teacher. In neither case does much critical, scholarly or interpretative thinking take place. Teachers need to provide a rich range of opportunities that facilitate open-ended learning and thinking processes.

One brief example comes from a Year 10 class which studied the novel *Only the Heart* by Brian Caswell and David Phu An Chiem in a traditional way with much face-to-face interaction in the classroom. Open-ended response tasks were then offered with the proviso that if students did not like the choices, they could make up their own topic. Subjects for response included:

- *Draw the Vo family tree, using Inspiration[7] software. Show the relationships between the characters and add paragraphs in Add Note to say what you know about each.*
- *Explore the topic 'Attitudes to War'. Use a concept map to tease out this topic in your own way.*
- *Choose any passage which is a clear description of a person or event from the novel. Put it into your Word Document, either by typing it in or by scanning it in or by reading it into a sound file. Now annotate the passage with Callout boxes or using the Add Note function or a verbal explanation in a second sound file, or respond in some other way.*
- *Interview a Vietnam veteran or a Vietnamese person who was in Vietnam at the time of the war or someone involved in the Vietnam protest movement or someone who has strong opinions about Australia's involvement in the war in Vietnam or someone who has something to say about our treatment of Vietnam veterans or some other person who will elucidate your understanding of the novel. Summarise the interview in a maximum of six PowerPoint slides to present orally to the class.*

- *Compile or compose theme music for each of the three sections of the novel. Accompany each with a key quote, visual representation and annotation to explain your choices.*
- *Create a photo story to show the main events in the novel. Use a maximum of ten pictures and give each a caption and annotated explanation.*

The range of choices built in here was used to extend the talented students, directing their choice to the more demanding tasks, while at the same time encouraging those who needed modified work by including some less challenging tasks but expecting them to do more of them. It also gave an opportunity to students with artistic or literary or musical skills to use them to enhance their responses and cross the subject barriers.

Classroom management and expectations

Computers of any kind in the classroom demand that we rethink the very basics of classroom management we were taught in our undergraduate courses. This could be as simple as ensuring that bags and power cords are carefully tucked under desks so that they are not a hazard to the teacher or anyone else moving around the room. It could mean ergonomically designed chairs with adjustable heights and wheels, so that students can roll across the room to the whiteboard or easily gather in groups away from the lure of the computer screen so they can focus on discussion.

These modifications may not be possible because many of us teach large classes in impossibly small rooms, or the wiring of rooms may not have been designed by teachers, who have to make the spaces work educationally and practically. Recent advances in cordless, wireless connectivity and better laptop battery life are alleviating these physical problems to some extent.

I have also found significant difficulty in checking work submissions. In the past, I could stand at the classroom door and collect written homework or a class task as students left the room, dealing with recalcitrants on the spot. Now if I ask for work to be sent by e-mail or lodged electronically and later find that it is not there, the student seems to have a plethora of excuses such as, 'I must have sent it to the wrong address', or 'Do you really know how to open an attachment?' or 'Perhaps the network wasn't up when I lodged it'. New ways of discipline, checking student files and keeping students on task are simply added challenges for teachers these days.

Some Deputy Heads, who happily follow up graffiti or smoking offences or punctuality issues, seem hesitant to take on board inappropriate material on a student computer file or the misuse of the school network, sometimes even leaving these issues to the IT technicians to unearth and deal with. At the very least, our discipline leaders may need the technician with them as they confront the student and unearth the offending material. One Head I know brings together the technician, the student and the parent to view inappropriate material

**Management initiatives:
Who leads the renaissance
in your school?**

which the student has accessed. This has a salutary effect!

Web discussions[8] can be a particularly fraught area of classroom management with secondary students unless they are tightly set up and carefully controlled. Anonymity of contribution in a large group may offer an opportunity for extroverts to show off and quiet students to retreat, so that the learning outcomes can be minimal, even if the potential is educationally limitless. Although Web discussion can rarely capture the immediacy and fiery interaction of a good classroom debate, it does give the students – especially the quieter ones, slower thinkers and ESL students – an opportunity to have a say and reflect on their answers before pressing the 'send' button.

Factors quite beyond the control of the teacher

My third and final area for teacher concern is the need for teachers to recognise that there are some things we have no control over, any more than we could stop the photocopier from breaking down. The best laid plans can be sabotaged by a flaky network or technicians who do not seem to support what teachers are trying to do, or by poorly maintained machines. We do not live in a perfect world and there will always be a need for 'Plan B' when any kind of technology is involved, but we also need to recognise that good IT technicians are people who have undergone specialised training, and that they often have different personalities

to the Science lab staff or Art or Home Economic aides teachers have been used to working with in the past.

Generally, we are familiar with teacher aides working near the staff offices and teaching spaces, readily available for communication with teachers, aware of the academic program and with clear lines of responsibility to the Heads of Faculty, who can direct and evaluate their work so that they are well tuned in to support the curriculum. By contrast, our IT technicians often work in an inaccessible area behind security doors and windows for very good reasons, surrounded by an apparent fog of jargon and mystery. Few seem to be aware of the details of curriculum and what kind of support teachers need, and can often be critical of teacher incompetence in the IT area. Teachers too are critical because they believe that technicians focus on tweaking or modifying the network and delivering clever solutions to problems that don't relate to educational outcomes.

One of the major problems, as I see it, is that very few system managers are accountable to anyone, from the Principal down, who is able to assess the technical details and competence of their work. Even school bursars, whose work is a mystery to most teachers, generally have a financial wizard on the school council who keeps a supportive eye on their work and are also subject to an independent external review each year when the auditors are called in. Rarely are such accountability or support mechanisms available to IT managers, yet they may spend millions of dollars over several years on the network, systems and associated hardware.

I see no simple or quick solution to this problem, which is common in many schools. If, however, the vision of the school includes an unambiguous statement on the value of ICT as an essential learning and thinking tool for this generation of students, then the mission statement of the school must include achievable objectives or strategies for the fulfillment of the vision. This can only happen if specific goals are agreed on together by the IT and academic staff, rather than the two groups holding each other at arm's length. Specific strategies must be agreed on between the groups as they acknowledge the need to work together as a team in achieving shared goals. This may require some skilful leadership and mediation by the Principal or Curriculum Coordinator.

Among the many schools that I have visited and the many teachers I have talked to, there is one school that seems to have a framework of management that could serve as a useful model for others. In this low-fee but 'compulsory laptop' school, the System Manager and the Director of E-Learning sit together in the same office, work through budgeting, networking, staff training and curriculum implementation goals together, and are both equally and jointly responsible for the implementation of these to the Deputy Headmaster.[9] The network at this school is rarely 'down'; there is a quick turnaround on laptop maintenance for students with only minimal inhouse technical staff. The Director of E-Learning is not IT-trained, nor does she claim to be a 'tech wiz', but she does have a strong belief that being in an environment with good intranet connectivity can enrich the learning experiences of her students and, by her classroom example, gives the teachers a clear understanding of what the school's IT policy is, why students are required to buy laptops and how they are to implement the policy in their classrooms.

It seems to me to be a very workable pattern on which to build school administrative structures and sound classroom management practices that will make the best use of the great potential of ICT.

Management initiatives:
Who leads the renaissance
in your school?

Endnotes

Sections of this chapter were first published as 'Classroom management challenges of notebook computing', edition of *Global Educator Newsletter*, May 2004, a higher education Web publication of monthly peer reviewed papers on issues relating to the IT global education classroom. See http://www.globaled.com/articles/DavidNettlebeck2004.pdf

[1] M. Fullan & A. Hargreaves, *What's worth fighting for in your school?* Teachers College Press, Columbia University, NY, 1992.

[2] B. Schneiderman, *Leonardo's laptop: human needs and the new computing technologies*, MIT Press, Cambridge Massachusetts, 2003, p. x.

[3] A. Goodwyn, 'What is the relationship between ICT, literacy and subject teaching and learning in a secondary school?' Paper presented at the International Federation for the Teaching of English, July 2003.

[4] R. Andrews, University of York, UK. Seminar presented at ACER Melbourne, July 2003 on some early findings of research on the impact of ICT on literacy learning.

[5] T. Brabazon, *Digital hemlock: Internet education and the poisoning of teaching*, UNSW Press, Sydney, 2002, p. 115.

[6] D. Lyon, 'Would God use e-mail?' in *Zadok Perspectives*, No. 71, Winter 2001.

[7] See details of this software in Appendix 2, p. 157.

[8] This area of the management of online discussions is dealt with more fully in Chapter 6, p. 67.

[9] Reference is to the management structure at Donvale Christian College, Melbourne.

Chapter 2

'Give up the idea that the pace of change will slow down ... It is not the pace of change that weighs us down; it is the piecemeal-ness and fragmentation that weighs us down ... All of us can change the immediate context around us and this leads us down the path to transformation.'[1]

The new paradigm for literacy:
Practical consequences for the classroom

The changing literacy framework

Teachers today are being forced to rethink the meaning of the terms 'literacy' and 'literacy education'. Traditional printed text as a primary means of communication, learning and information storage and transfer is rapidly being superseded. Technology is therefore shifting the ways in which people learn and communicate. It is more common for us to find students channel hopping, Net-surfing, multi-tasking and thinking in mosaics rather than reading a printed book. 'The post-literate generation is making the shift from word to image, from text to hypertext and from single sources to the interconnectedness of word, image and sound.'[2]

Traditional English teachers would like to anchor their ships in the safe harbour of literature and cling to the now moribund cultural heritage model of learning rather than venture out into an anarchic and largely untravelled world where the living culture is the 'culture of the computer, the Internet, the global media, the hypertext, the interactive encyclopaedia and of course the book'.[3] It is not a case of yet another trick in the teacher's toolbag. Prain and Lyons show us that technologies are not just add-on resources but that 'technological practices and capabilities are changing significantly what counts as literacy and how this literacy might be learnt'.[4]

Brenton Doecke puts it this way:
The social world that teenagers inhabit forms a vital frame of reference for the reading, writing, speaking and listening that happen in English classrooms. English enables students to focus on how language shapes their lives, from the language of newspapers and television advertisements, to the imaginative worlds of novels, sitcoms and movies.[5]

In his article 'Defining new literacies in curricular practice', Ladislaus M Semali[6] helpfully summarises the 'new literacies' as those that have emerged in the post-typographic era. He believes that, as a consequence, teachers must examine their assumptions about reading, writing and books. To help them do this, he identifies five literacies in the course of the article: **computer literacy**, which is simply competence with visual representations, visual literacy and interactivity ('competencies needed to perform a variety of tasks related to computer language and use'); **information literacy**, where students have 'the ability to recognize when information is needed and … to locate, evaluate, and use effectively needed information'; **media literacy**, which he defines as 'as the ability to access, experience, evaluate, and produce media products', and where students have the ability 'to sift through the variety of presentations, including films, newspapers, Web sites, and video screens to arrive at meaning'; **television literacy**, where students can 'read and interpret television messages including advertising'; and **visual literacy**, which he says is 'an interdisciplinary concept that includes theoretical perspectives, visual language perspectives, presentational perspectives, and technological development, including digitization'.

Impact of computer **technologies**

In the light of all that is going on around us, we have no choice but to recognise that the new information and computer technologies undergird much of the social and educational context in which we now find ourselves. Our children grow up in this environment and experience the world differently because of it. Even for preschool children, the use of a computer may precede the use of pen and paper to form letters. Research tells us that 75 per cent of children begin using a computer before the age of four and many acquire the skills of reading and writing on a computer screen at the same time as they are learning to write with pen and paper.[7] This can lead, among other things, to a huge gulf between teacher and student. For many teachers, ICT can be a foreign world they are learning to cope with, rather than a natural part of life they have grown up with. For students, therefore, their online world becomes almost a private biosphere where the language, imagery and ethos may be increasingly divorced from their school world and the culture of their teachers.

There is also a factor of both overt and covert parental influence with the use of technology in the classroom. One-to-one computing in some schools appears to increase and reinforce the alienation between the generations. This may begin with the simple notion that parents can no longer look over the shoulders of the child and see what homework is being done. Deliberate steps need to be taken, perhaps at information evenings, parent classes or parent–teacher interviews in order to remove the mystery of ICT-generated work and to encourage continued interaction and openness at home.

Centrality of teacher's role

At a time when we fear that we are watching the apparent demise of our book-centred culture, we must strongly reaffirm the centrality of the teacher's role in providing for engaged and effective learning with and through information and communications technology. Catherine Beavis reminds us that it is still our fundamental concern to find

> *ways for students to become highly engaged and reflectively, critically literate … to develop high levels of literary competence, understanding and expertise in their subject areas … for there to be powerful and self-evident links between students' present and future in and out of school worlds …*[8]

Richard Andrews, Professor of Education at York, summarises the current situation as follows:

> *Because word processing is second nature to us now … it is easy to take for granted what digital composing has done for us. It has enabled concentration on the major structuring of writing; enabled argument, report and information writing to have a better medium for their expression than pen and paper; encouraged collaboration and talk about writing at the screen; liberated and validated drafting and editing; and improved presentation. On the down side, it has made many learners dependent on spelling and grammar checkers; been overrated in its effect on narrative writing; limited a sense of the whole work through its window onto a*
> *text; and in some cases led to a deterioration in handwriting quality.*[9]

The various elements of ICT offer us powerful ways of working with language. There are, however, many despairing teachers who find it difficult to see beyond the perceived pressure of the pen and paper examinations that currently drive the system at the top end. They catalogue limited access to equipment, the hijacking of facilities by ICT classes, poor online access, self-serving technical support in some schools, and the fear of an over-simplistic view of the internet as the new fetish in teaching or even the ridiculous hyperbole peddled by 'snake-oil' salespeople about computers as the panacea for educational ills.

In the light of this, it is reassuring to read of research in the United Kingdom, which found that only one-fifth of teachers were in the 'fearful' category – those who see computers as alienating, bewildering, threatening and anti-social, and who continue to say 'books have to be central' and 'you just cannot get away from pen and paper'. About a third of the teachers in the study had mixed feelings, but saw computers as a motivator, especially for the less able and reluctant boys. However, this group did express serious concerns about students losing their social skills.

Just over half the teachers now felt optimistic. They felt that 'ICT was empowering and stimulating, providing genuinely new forms of communication and means of gaining information and access to texts of all kinds … that it broadens the whole concept of literacy …'[10]

Of course, reading and writing are still basic skills, but the way we teach and the way children learn is changing. The newsletter of the Australian Literacy Educators Association argues that the current multiliteracies environment means that

our personal, public and working lives are changing in some dramatic ways, and these ways are transforming our cultures and the ways we communicate. This means that the way we have taught literacy, and what counts for literacy, will also have to change.[11]

Ilana Snyder from Monash University sums up the situation from her tertiary perspective by saying that education

is at a 'critical crossroad. Language and literacy educators have within their power the opportunity to shift their own and their students' beliefs and understandings about the new technologies … and this process is now happening.'[12] Computers can be a transformative tool which will enable us to think and act in a whole new way about teaching and learning. Di McDonald, in her recent research, says:

Most computer software is now non-linear, highly individualized, provides multiple representations of reality, emphasizes knowledge construction and often, as in simulations, provides real world and case-based learning. These software elements appear to be based more on constructivist theories of learning than behaviourist theories.[13]

Taking advantage **of flexibility**

It will be no panacea, but there is certainly light on the horizon for those willing to see it, experiment and evaluate. The focus of communication in schools is still on the written word, whether on screen or paper, so students with language difficulties are still at a disadvantage, although perhaps more motivated in this new learning culture. Students for whom learning was never a priority will be no more careful about maintaining their laptops or caring for their backups or floppy discs than they

ever were with folders, text books, paper and pens. Students with poor organisational skills are no better with computers than they were with paper folders. They still need the ability to organise and retrieve files and 'adequate literacy skills to read and understand information, the writing skills to communicate with others, and the personal management skills to remain focused on their learning'.[14]

On the other side of the coin, students can now move easily between paper and screen with the enormous advantage of easy drafting and revision to improve meaning and the ability to incorporate the texts of others into their writing. There is also the potential for interactive composing between students, just as is the norm in many offices and institutions outside the school. Few students have ever been original thinkers, but we should perhaps be more conscientious than ever before in our teaching of the need for careful referencing and acknowledgement of sources.

The purpose of this chapter was not to be a treatise on the changing nature of literacy and the role of the teacher, but to set the scene briefly for the practical suggestions which follow. What we cannot do is to pretend that the changing experiences and world view of students can be ignored in the classroom. Marion Meiers, who edits *Literacy and Learning in The Middle Years* for the Australian Literacy Educators Association, said in a recent article,

The conversations that will engage teachers and their students in articulating new theories, including a theory of the visual and verbal, will be complex, provocative and even daunting, but in the end, we will have once again incorporated changes into the study of texts in English.[15]

Hopefully this book will contribute to this ongoing conversation.

Endnotes

Some sections of this chapter were presented as a keynote address in the 21st Century Literacies strand at the International Federation for the Teaching of English conference, Melbourne, July 2003, and subsequently published as D. Nettelbeck, 'ICT and the reshaping of literacy: a secondary classroom perspective', in the joint publication *English in Australia*, No. 139/*Literacy Learning: the Middle Years*, Vol. 12, No. 1, February 2004.

1 M. Fullan, *Leading in a culture of change*, Jossey-Bass, San Francisco, 2001.

2 G. Kelly, *Retrofuture: rediscovering our roots, recharting our routes*, InterVarsity Press, Illinois, 1999. Includes a fuller discussion on the post-literate generation: Chapter 6, 'Gutenberg and Fries'.

3 A. Goodwyn (ed.), *English in the digital age: information and communications technology and the teaching of English*, Cassell, London, 2000, p. 5.

4 V. Prain & L. Lyons, 'Using information and communication technologies in English: an Australian perspective', in A. Goodwyn (ed.), 2000, op. cit.

5 B. Doecke, 'Is anybody listening?', *EQ Australia*, No. 1, Autumn, 2004.

6 M. Semali, *Defining new literacies in curricular practice*, *Reading Online*, viewed 7 January 2003, <http://www.readingonline.org/newliteracies/semali1/index.html>

7 Meredith, Russell, Blackwood, Thomas & Wise, *Real time: computers, change and schooling*, available at http://abs.gov.au 2000, quoted in C. Durrant & C. Beavis, *P(ICT)URES of ENGLISH – Teachers, learners and technology*, Australian Association for the Teaching of English, Adelaide, 2001, p. 213.

8 C. Beavis, 'Critical engagement: literacy, curriculum and ICTs' in *Idiom – Journal of the Victorian Association for the Teaching of English*, Vol. 38, No. 2, Sept 2002.

9 R. Andrews, 'Framing and design in ICT in English: towards a new subject and new practices in the classroom,' in A. Goodwyn (ed.), 2000, op. cit., p. 23.

10 ibid., p. 8.

11 B. Cope & M. Kalantzis, 'Putting "Multiliteracies" to the test', *Newsletter of the Australian Literacy Educators Association*, February 2001.

12 I. Snyder, 'The new communication order', in C. Durrant & C. Beavis, 2001, op. cit.

13 D. McDonald, 'Hypertext and historical literacy', doctoral thesis under preparation, Monash University, 2004.

14 J. Misko, 'On-line learning in the knowledge-based society: a VET perspective', *Unicorn*, Journal of the Australian College of Education, Vol. 28, No. 3, December 2002.

15 M. Meiers, 'Then and now: texts in the English classroom', *EQ Australia*, No. 1, Autumn 2004.

Chapter 3

'Technology is neither an end in itself nor an add on. It is a tool for improving ... and ultimately transforming teaching and learning.'[1]

Concept mapping:
ICT as a learning and thinking tool

The learning and thinking context

Drawing concept maps is not a new activity for students. Such maps can represent knowledge in a visual way and are useful for planning and brainstorming ideas, with links identifying the relationships between the concepts, characters or themes. An early developer of the technique in the 1960s was Professor Joseph D. Novak at Cornell University, New York. He argued that concept maps are effective because 'meaningful learning involves the assimilation of new concepts and propositions into existing cognitive structures'.[2]

A group of colleagues in a school using laptop computers were concerned that students' notebook computers should be much more than glorified word processors. They saw them as a potential new way of fostering excellence and innovation, as well as an opportunity to challenge existing classroom practices, which at that time did little more than put what was on paper onto the computer screen. Burford and Cooper called this 'new approaches to teaching and learning, ... [using] the strengths and limitations of different technologies, catering to different styles of learning

and designing effective learning environments [that] require a new set of skills'.[3]

This development is closely allied to the constructivist theory of learning, where the learner is an active participant and the students' responses are valued, even when they differ from the teacher's perspective. Students construct understanding that is meaningful to them and explore a range of possibilities. Constructivist teachers 'use primary sources, along with manipulative, interactive ... materials'.[4] They also seek elaboration of students' initial responses and provide time for students to 'construct relationships and create metaphors'. Many will be familiar with the work of Seymour Papert[5] and Logo – a computer program that encourages students to think. Inspiration[6] software, and the use of other onscreen concept maps, provides another type of virtual thinking tool that enables 'the learner [to construct] his/her own world picture [reality] from individual experience'.[7]

In a more recent and very challenging article, Professor Brian Caldwell argued that 'nurturing and sustaining a culture of innovation is critical to

Concept mapping:
ICT as a learning
and thinking tool

the transformation of schools'.[8] Under the pressure of time and discipline constraints, it is so comfortable to revert to the traditional linear essay or standardised test. In the same journal, Andy Hargreaves warns that we could so easily capitulate to the task of maintaining order, teaching to the test and following standardised curriculum scripts, thus becoming the 'drones and clones of policy makers … anaemic ambitions for whatever under-funded systems can achieve'. However, he poses the alternative of a high investment, high capacity educational system, in which 'highly skilled teachers are able to generate creativity and ingenuity among their pupils …'[9] Concept mapping is only one way to do this but it is an easily accessible way and one that students respond to very positively.

Classroom strategies

The following examples demonstrate how one group of colleagues took the first tentative steps along this very exciting road.

Concept mapping task – a Year 11 online examination

Linear essays have been the staple of classroom practice and examinations for many generations. They can be efficient, but take time to plan and write, are tedious to mark and favour only one style of thinking. Often ideas are obfuscated by a student who plans poorly or sets out to hide ignorance. Of course, the planning and writing of an essay is still an important skill, but what a range of other response possibilities we now have available to us!

Inspiration software not only allows the students to create a concept map but to manipulate it. They can 'write' in the concept boxes or use the 'Add Note' function as a separate, yet linked writing space. They can also manipulate the shape, placement, colour and size of the concept boxes, making their maps highly individualistic. They can label and move the links. This software allows a high degree of manipulation and the students can easily change and modify what they have done as they make their links and associations. It is a powerful visual learning tool that inspires students to develop ideas and organise their thinking.

We wanted our students to create a 'clustering' concept map in which they were asked to begin with a main idea, in this case a quotation from *Heart of Darkness*, the classic novel by Joseph Conrad. They were then asked to generate other ideas around it relating to the characters, prose, symbols, themes and narrative. We anticipated that their maps would be essentially non-linear. The links between the ideas would be explained and they would be able to make connections and possibly new associations between the various elements of the novel. We expected the students to be able to show and explain the relationships in the novel. Hopefully, they would create links and cross-links that could be rich in meaning. It was a noble ideal! Did it work?

After classroom practice, we asked students under examination conditions and in less than 30 minutes, to respond to any one of five quotes from *Heart of Darkness*. The task was open-ended in that they were required to explore the topic in at least four ways, identify in the links the relationship between the quote and the concepts, and then to write up to 300 words as notes behind the boxes. Below is the response of one student:

The notes for this student behind the box labelled 'Journey of the Self' were:

The trip upstream was called 'Journey into the Heart of Darkness' for not only was it a journey into Africa but into the soul.

The Doctor told Marlow before he left, 'The changes take place inside you know.' While it is easy to claim that the Africans had 'horrid ways', Marlow claimed that all men had the susceptibility to go wild. In Africa there was no judgement over what the whites did. Kurtz adopted the savage ways, putting heads on spears as trophies. There were no limitations put in place. So while the 'cannibals' may have been savage, the whites also murdered, pillaged and remained guilt-free.

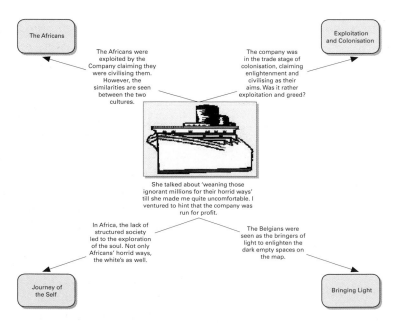

Diagram created in Inspiration® by Inspiration Software®, Inc.

Concept mapping:
ICT as a learning
and thinking tool

How do we assess this kind of response?

Here are the criteria we devised:

Criteria	5	4	3	2	1
Knowledge of the text					
Clarity and relevance of the links					
Control of the mechanics of language					
Complexity of ideas and issues explored					

This exercise was surprisingly quick to mark and we found it very easy to sort out those who did from those who did not understand the fundamentals of the novel. It was also open-ended, so that no two responses were remotely similar. Most students demonstrated quite innovative thinking to a greater degree than would have been possible within the confines of an essay format. The writing in the links used a specific telegraphic mode of literacy where the students could encapsulate understanding in a particularly concise way.

It was soon evident that some students did not know the text. This 'virtual' task did not hide their lack of knowledge in the 'colour and movement' that is one of the attractions of the Inspiration software. Our verbose essay writers, more often girls, could no longer hide behind a flurry of words. Our creative but disorganised students, more often boys, took their diagrams in various directions but sometimes found it hard to clinch what they wanted to communicate.

What did we achieve?

Some quite exciting creative thinking was demonstrated by students, who, while not particularly talented at writing linear, argumentative essays, 'unpacked' the topic in some remarkable ways. They had clearly understood the intertextuality of *Heart of Darkness* and demonstrated this understanding quickly and succinctly. All 150 Year 11 students completed the task in the 30 minutes that were allocated. There were no software failures or suggestions of unfairness because it was not a traditional pen and paper essay test. Many expressed their delight in being able to organise their response in such a different way. The range of marks was as wide as an essay response, but with some different students at the top and bottom of the range.

As in Gardner's theory of multiple intelligences, perhaps this form of response provided those students who are visual/spatial learners with an opportunity to shine in English, where normally the verbal/linguistic students perform the best. The former 'wrote' the information more pictorially (as indeed they can with other multimedia authoring tools), although Inspiration did allow the verbal/linguistic students to do what they do best – 'write' fluently and effectively in the note boxes, where we suggested a desirable word limit.

Establishing the characters and concepts in a text

A quite different use of Inspiration software is as a discussion tool early on in the study of a text, to ensure that the major characters and their relationships are understood. In this example, several Year 10 students worked together in a group to develop the following concept map to help them sort out who was who in Shakespeare's *Twelfth Night*.

As an alternative to a traditional essay response, a Year 7 class was asked to show their understanding of the relationships between characters in a novel in the form of a concept map. In the example below, a Year 7 student has used an Inspiration map to sort out the relationships in a *Harry Potter* story. The significant advantage of this kind of work is the requirement to name the links, as this forces the student to enunciate the relationships. They found it an enjoyable experience. It was quick to do as it took only one homework period, included visual and colour elements, and the student could write brief notes behind each character box:

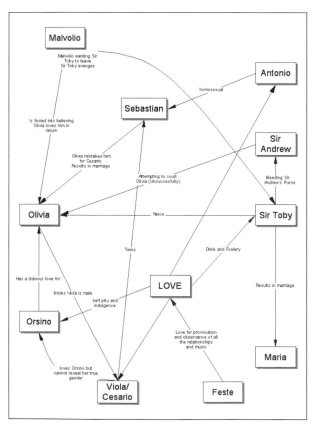

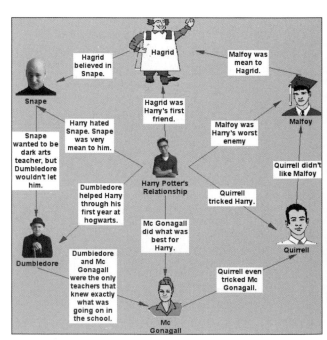

Diagrams created in Inspiration® by Inspiration Software®, Inc.

Concept mapping:
ICT as a learning
and thinking tool

This student's notes behind the Snape icon are:

> Snape is the meanest teacher there ever was and ever will be. He walks around picking on people and trying to find someone doing the wrong thing.
>
> Snape only picks on kids that aren't in Sletheren. He picks on Harry the most even though he saved his life.

It would have been a tedious experience indeed for a 12-year-old to get all this information into an essay form and even more tedious for the teacher to mark it, yet as a classroom exercise we could see very quickly who did and who did not understand the key concepts in the text, giving us a basis upon which to develop further teaching.

In similar vein, Year 8 students developed quite complex character maps from the novel *The Hobbit*. Their starting point was the requirement to explore the ideas of good and evil and to develop their understanding of the characters in relation to this. Instead of using the library of clip art in the program, they imported actual film stills from the film's web site. Part of the map and text which one student developed is shown below. (Film stills have not been reproduced for copyright reasons.)

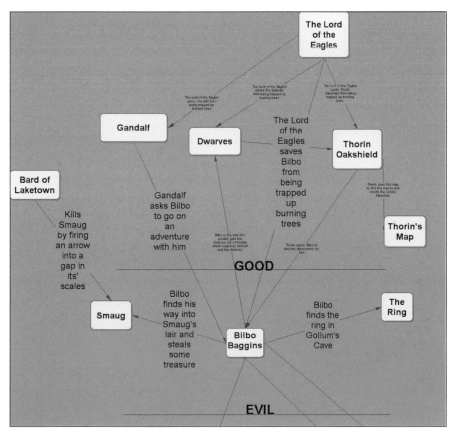

Diagram created in Inspiration® by Inspiration Software®, Inc.

Concept mapping as a planning tool

In a Year 10 assessment task on the film text *The Truman Show*, students were required to use Inspiration software to plan their essay.

The rubric for the task was:

a   Open a new Inspiration Document.

b   In the main box, put in the topic you have chosen.

c   Create at least four new boxes, one for each aspect of the topic you will explore in the essay. Into each box, put the idea or concept that you will examine in each paragraph. These will form the ideas for the paragraphs of the essay.

d   Use the Add Note function for each circle to put in dot point form what you may say in that paragraph.

e   Use the links to write the topic sentence for each paragraph.

f   In the Add Note function behind the Main box, draft your opening paragraph.

g   After 30 minutes but not earlier, open a new Word Document and write your essay.

Below is the plan that one student submitted. Note how he has copied the topic into the main box, while aspects that he aims to deal with are listed in the four surrounding sub-boxes. These will become paragraphs in the essay and the topic sentence for each paragraph is ready in the link to the sub-box.

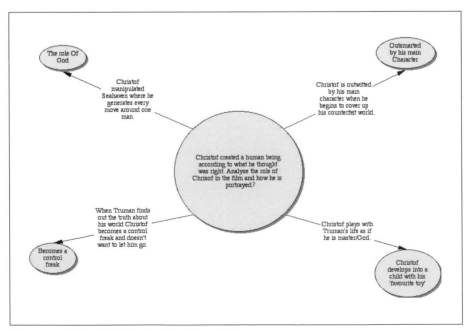

The role Of God

Outsmarted by his main Character

Christof manipulated Seahaven where he generates every move around one man.

Christof is outwitted by his main character when he begins to cover up his counterfeit world.

Christof created a human being according to what he thought was right. Analyse the role of Chrisof in the film and how he is portrayed?

When Truman finds out the truth about his world Christof becomes a control freak and doesn't want to let him go.

Christof plays with Truman's life as if he is master/God.

Becomes a control freak

Christof develops into a child with his 'favourite toy'

Diagram created in Inspiration® by Inspiration Software®, Inc.

Concept mapping:
ICT as a learning
and thinking tool

For the aspect, 'Outsmarted by his main character', the notes behind the circle were as follows:

> Christof is outwitted by his main character when he begins to cover up his counterfeit world.
>
> – Truman realises the simulated world he is living in.
> – Gets his first ideas from Sylvia who informs him on the beach.
> – He outwits Christof by thinking that someone is watching his every move.
> – Finds the courage to go out to sea as his father has returned and never died.
> – It shows that Christof tries to predict what Truman is thinking.

From this basic planning and preliminary thinking, it was then simple for this student to write the opening paragraph, followed by the entire essay in about 30 minutes.

What did we achieve?

The students seemed to think through the topic more carefully using this tool and structured their final responses more thoroughly because they had to plan in this way. Our only concern was that students who became used to thinking and drafting on screen might find it difficult later to transfer those skills to the less flexible world of paper when the time came for a formal examination.

Science, history and religious education examples

This software has applications across all faculties. In the example below, a Year 8 Science teacher asked students to summarise their understanding of the carbon cycle:[10]

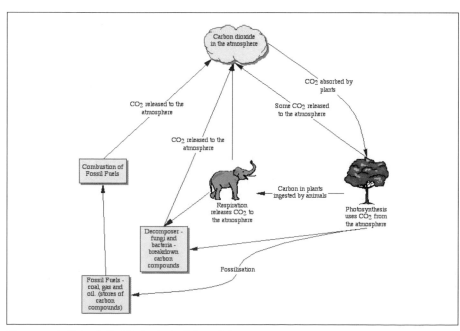

Diagram created in Inspiration® by Inspiration Software®, Inc.

In another Science class, this student used Inspiration as a revision tool to organise her knowledge of the optics unit.

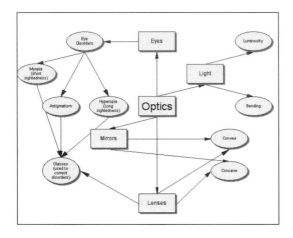

In this Year 9 History class, the students worked in groups to try to sort out their hazy understanding of the Australian federal government system. This is just part of the map one group developed:

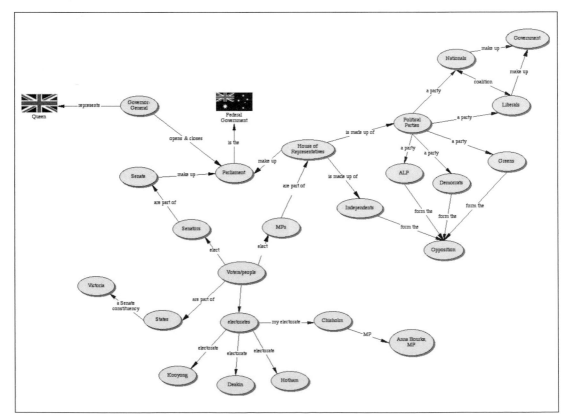

Diagrams created in Inspiration® by Inspiration Software®, Inc.

Concept mapping:
ICT as a learning
and thinking tool

In a Year 10 Religious Education class studying a unit on Sacred Texts, with emphasis on the two creation stories in Genesis, the teacher established the conceptual framework by first teaching them the history and geography of the ancient Middle East. The outcome from this section was peer-assessed after students prepared short PowerPoint presentations which included maps, diagrams and other graphics. For the study of the concepts of one God, faithfulness, revelation, covenant, promise and so on, the students summarised their understanding in a concept map using Inspiration software. After the text analysis section of the work, the students annotated a section of the passage as they had a copy of the Bible on their laptops, but they were also encouraged to annotate a work of art that illustrated some aspect of the creation story. For this, they searched one of the many art museums from around the world online. Their final understanding of these scripture texts was summarised in a traditional essay.[11]

Nothing outlined above is particularly innovative or difficult to achieve, but it does require a measure of collegial support and a risk-taking culture within the school. Exploring new ways of teaching can be an exciting challenge.

There is no suggestion that we abandon essay writing, as this is still an important skill and one that is strongly valued in high stakes mass testing, particularly as a hurdle for tertiary entrance. What this kind of learning does is to stimulate ideas, challenge conventional thinking and hopefully prepare students in a far better way for the narrow gateway of written examinations. It may also make learning more open-ended and, therefore, more exciting.

Endnotes

Sections of this chapter were first published as D. Nettelbeck & D. McDonald, 'Mapping the heart of darkness: using Inspiration software to explore the inter-textuality of Conrad's Heart of Darkness during a Year 11 on-line examination' in *Opinion* – Journal of the SA English Teachers Association. Vol. 45, No. 1, Term 2, 2001.

[1] Mission Statement – Lin Wood Public Schools, New Hampshire, veiwed 28 May 2004, <http://www.lin-wood.k12.nh.us/documents/public/technology.htm>

[2] J. Novak, *The concept mapping*, Homepage, viewed 3 December 2000, <http://www.to.utwente.nl/user/ism/lanzing/cm_home.htm>

[3] S. Burford & L. Cooper, 'Online development using WebCT: A faculty managed process for quality', *Australian Journal of Educational Technology*, Vol. 16, No. 3, Summer 2000, p. 208.

[4] J. Brooks & M. Brooks, 'Constructivist classrooms', viewed 3 December 2004, <htttp://129.7.160.15/inst5931/constructivist.html>

[5] S. Papert, *The children's machine*, Harper Collins, New York, 1993.

[6] See Appendix 2 for details.

[7] *Education and Technology Convergence*, Commissioned Report No. 43, January, 1996. National Board of Employment, Education and Training. Australian Government Publishing Service, p. 84.

[8] *Snapshots: The Specialist Schools Trust Journal of Innovation in Education*, UK, Vol. 1, No 1, July 2003, Editorial p. 2.

[9] A. Hargreaves, 'Teaching in the knowledge society', *Snapshots: The Specialist Schools Trust Journal of Innovation in Education*, Vol. 1, No. 1, July 2003, pp. 7–10.

[10] Prepared by Harry Leather when teaching at St Michaels Grammar School.

[11] Unit of work developed by Rowan Swaney, Geelong Grammar School.

Chapter 4

'Few teachers see technology as a goal in itself. They want to see how technology might make their students better writers, readers and thinkers. They don't care much whether they are good word processors.'[1]

Annotation:

A focus on close reading of the text

The learning and thinking context

Suppliers of educational software often promote their material as 'interactive' when it may be little more than words onscreen. Some teachers believe that they have 'computerised' their courses and work entirely online, when what they often mean is that all their notes and course material have been scanned into a computer and students have exactly the same material onscreen as appeared on paper, albeit more colourful and internally indexed. Beware the electronic shovel! The new, so-called interactive work may be just the same learning tasks and notes delivered in a different format.

This can be a particular pitfall in schools which have invested in expensive software as front-end organisers. Teachers and students may find that the original resources have simply been transferred from one medium to another without any change in the nature or demands of the learning.

It seems so easy with computers to churn out yet another worksheet which smart students complete too quickly and find boring, while struggling students fail to cope with it and invent yet another avoidance strategy. Study guides or commercially produced study notes can easily become the curse of the senior secondary student. For them, it seems so much simpler to buy a summary and notes about the text than to read it and respond to the direct voice of the writer.

In this context, Richard Andrews reminds us that we are moving away from the text as a stable, fixed, cultural artefact. A student can now

play with Shakespeare, by, for example, inter-cutting his text with yours, editing his words, writing new speeches and lines, commenting alongside his words in the same font … In such a world, reading becomes a creative act, and the processes of composition apply to both reading and writing, interpreting and making.[2]

In the same vein, Andrew Goodwyn provides this perspective:

… ideas about, in a sense, interfering with the text of others, are aimed at increasing students' understanding of how texts work by getting inside them … what the electronic text offers them is the opportunity to get inside the text and to enhance it or contest it from within … We should be cynical about some of the claims for 'computer literacy' but we should

Annotation:
A focus on
close reading
of the text

also be idealistic about the power that students can now have over texts, their own and those of others.[3]

Here, computers are not simply used as word processors, where students can easily redraft their work and quickly complete comprehension exercises or quiz questions on poems. We are talking about productive learning engagement, ongoing cerebral challenge and increasing the range and 'depth of intellectual processing'.[4] Computers can help us to deepen the texture of learning with processes 'which are otherwise unavailable to students in classrooms.

This aspect of online content appears to provide the most potential for improving learning and understanding'.[5] The best learning does not occur when we ask students to find the tricks and skills in poetic devices or unravel the code or remember the rhyming pattern.

It happens when 'deep processing occurs through challenging and open-ended tasks'.[6] Computers help teachers do this more easily than was possible in the past.

In the study of poetry and the close analysis of a fiction or play text, computers offer the student genuine open-ended learning experiences with a range of intellectual processing that comes close to the best models of whole brain learning. Technology can enrich and broaden the study of and response to texts in ways that have never been possible up to now. The medium is still a fresh and attractive one to students, and most are delighted with the ability their computer gives them to present colourful and well laid-out work that genuinely reflects their individuality. This meshes with the personal and very individualistic nature of most literature, especially poetry.

Classroom strategies

Responses to poetry tasks

The following are several classroom practices tried by colleagues. Some are better suited to one kind of poem or a particular learning outcome than others, and as we developed these we have tried to be self-critical with each other about what actually worked.

Annotating with callout boxes

Students really enjoy annotating a poem with **callout boxes** from the Word/Drawing toolbar. When students have selected one poem that appeals to them for whatever reason, the instruction for a Year 8 or 9 class could be:

Annotate the poem. You will do this by using at least six callout boxes. In these callout boxes you will be writing a total of between 100 and 150 words of comment about the poem.

Here is part of the response of a
Year 9 student to Bruce Dawe's poem
'War Without End':

War Without End

This war was not like any other war,
it was world-wide, and it was never done,
thousands died each year, and thousands more
robbed of all sweetness underneath the sun.

The front-line ran through every road and street,
they died alone, in small groups (most were young),
no general offered up a balance-sheet
to justify torn limbs and silent tongue.

This war was not like any other war,
there was no enemy with a foreign face,
we could not see what all the fuss was for
– when someone died, it was some other place...

The rusting junk-yards were not on our maps,
the rehab hospitals off-limits too,
we could not ever imagine that perhaps
someday our wheels and us might join the queue.

And daily still, in sunshine and in rain,
the ambulances with their strident cries
sort out the barely living from the slain,
while, all invisibly, our future dies

Genghis Khan, it's said, composed a hill
of skulls as tribute to his conquering hand
– he knew what he was doing; when we kill
we can only say we do not understand.

A difference between this war and other war is that it is not a war fought between two countries or races. The casualties are mostly self-inflicted.

Driving is a risk. Maybe someday, we will crash. Our car will be dumped to the junkyards that are never seen on the map, and our bodies will probably be in the rehab hospitals. Both we and the car will be visiting a new, unknown place.

This is a metaphor, saying that every road and street is the front line. The soldiers – drivers and passengers – die alone or in small groups. The passage also states that most of the dead are young people, which also makes us think. Weren't most of our soldiers young?

This passage creates an image of the ambulances rushing to the site and trying to find any survivors. The nurses and doctors try to revive the seriously wounded, but most likely, the victims of this war will die, unseen.

Annotation:
A focus on
close reading
of the text

Callouts and graphics

Students also enjoy showing their understanding of a poem with pictures as well as words. In this example, the students were required to use callout boxes from the Word/Drawing toolbar but also the Insert Picture function from that tool bar. The rubric was:

Read this poem carefully three or four times until you are sure that you understand it well. Then respond to it in whatever way you wish, but you must include at least four notes and two sentences in each note and at least four pictures.

Here is part of the response of a Year 10 student to the song 'Only Nineteen'.[7] The lines he chose were highlighted in different colours and the connecting lines and explanatory text were in the same colours.

Document 2

On two legs; it was a war within yourself.

But you wouldn't let your mates down 'til they had you dusted off.

So you closed your eyes and thought about something else.

And then someone yelled out 'Contact!' and the bloke behind me swore.

We hooked in there for hours, then a god-almighty roar.

And Frankie kicked a mine the day that mankind kicked the moon.

God help me, he was going home in June.

I can still see Frankie drinking tinnies in the Grand Hotel.

On a thirty-six hour rec. leave in Vung Tau.

And I can still hear Frankie lying screaming in the jungle.

'Til the morphine came and killed the bloody row.

And the Anzac legends didn't mention mud and blood and tears.

And the stories that my Father told me never seemed quite real.

I caught some pieces in my back that I didn't even feel.

God help me, I was only nineteen.

And can you tell me doctor, why I still can't get to sleep?

And why the Channel 7 chopper chills me to my feet?

And what's this rash that comes and goes, can you tell me what it means?

God help me, I was only nineteen.

Australian War Memorial
Negative Number BEL/69/0378/VN

>

Document 2 cont'd

One of the only ways to get to Vietnam was by helicopter.

The bad memories of Vietnam can be brought back to people in Australia by the sound of a helicopter. This is because they went to Vietnam in helicopters and this brings back to them what happened there and how close they came to death.

A shot person is taken from Vietnam in a helicopter.

One of the only things that could save you if you got shot was a shot of morphine which would kill the pain until the helicopter came or you died. The shot of morphine could also relax your body so much that your heart stopped beating and you died. It was either a life saver or a death sentence. It was the only thing that could be done for someone hurt in the field.

Australian War Memorial
Negative Numbers: COL/67/0781/VN;
COL/67/0140/VN; FOD/71/0257/VN.

Much of the time was spent on the ground in the mud, shooting at an invisible enemy hiding in the jungle.

The stories the young kids heard from the Anzacs were about good times and heroes in the war, they never heard about the real face of war, the bodies, the bleeding and screaming of pain. Many people who went had no idea of what they would have to see. This would scar them for the rest of their lives.

Annotation:
A focus on
close reading
of the text

Use yellow sticky notes or Insert/Comment function

A simple but similar means of response preferred by some students is to annotate on screen with notes. In this case, the task was defined as:

Make a personal response to any aspects of this poem by using the footnote facility in 'Insert/Comment'. You should write at least six comments with one or two sentences of explanation in each.

The following two responses are from Year 9 students. The first was the result of a group discussion by three boys. The second was part of an assessment task, where students were given 30 minutes to respond to one of two unseen poems:

Document 3

Small-town dream

The back-roads school bus strains

past the side entrance of Blue's

Auto Repairs where three men slump

in startling white plastic chairs

in the eight-thirty am sun,

eyes delving into the depths

of mugs deep in sprawling hands.

Behind the safety net

of a casually curved arm

with ankle shackle of thumb & forefinger,

a determined small boy climbs toward

the Kosciuszko of his father's shoulder.

> 'Back roads' suggests the bus has come a long way over difficult country, straining around every corner.

> This is a dozy town where the men 'slump' in boredom while they gaze into the depths of mugs held in 'sprawling' workmans' hands.

> Chairs are 'startling white' because we perhaps expect everything in this little town to be dusty or dirty.

> The 'eight-thirty am sun' is bright and probably hot already – that is why the men gaze away into their mugs.

> Why is the father there? Is he one of the workers typical of a country town? Is the shackle a symbol of not being able to get away from the town?

> Strong metaphor of safety for the child – to him the father is vast and powerful like Mt Kosciuszko.

>

Document 3 cont'd

On the next gear-groaning corner

a weatherboard house has settled,

loose-limbed, against a river red gum.

In dusty shade

a slump-shouldered caravan

& three shambly old cars

with deflated tyres

sprawl in a gossiping circle

beside a shaggy camel, fostering flies,

ruminating on nothing – some

half-forgotten dreamship – hobbled

In the narrow yard.

Kathielyn Job

> Repetition of sounds – 'gear groaning', 'loose-limbed' and 'river red' give the reader an interesting pattern and rhythm.

> This is a picture of a run-down house, perhaps with paint peeling, propped up by the powerful tree.

> Like the wrecked cars with deflated tyres, the town isn't going anywhere – even the camel is old and looks depressed and diseased, covered in flies.

> The town is depressed and inward looking – even the camel which is 'dreamship' from another world, a 'ship of the desert' for escape, is now half-forgotten and is 'hobbled in the narrow yard', leaving us a negative picture of the town.

**Annotation:
A focus on
close reading
of the text**

Document 4

Bury Me

Bury me in a lotus pond
So that eels may swish by my ears,

The eels are alive and so represent that life and death is also in the present, so life and death co-exist together.

While on the lanterns – the green lotus leaves,
Fireflies flicker, now dim, now bright.

Light which is created by the fireflies is a symbol of birth or life but when the light disappears this symbolises death. Again, life and death co-exist.

Bury me under the acacia flowers
So I may have sweet dreams for ever

Acacia flowers produce eatable bulbs which are sweet and thus if you were to be buried under them, you would have 'sweet dreams'.

Or bury me on top of Mount T'ai
Where the wind wails over a lone pine.

The pine is alone but when the wind wails over, it is as if it is talking. When the person is dead and alone, he will be kept company by the 'wails' of the wind.

Or burn me to ashes and scatter me
In a river where spring tides are surging high,

Spring is a symbol of things coming to life such as plants flowering and showing their true beauty which was initially capsulated within the plant. This person really wants to turn his death, which is unpleasant, into something pleasant and wants to be with the things he/she finds beautiful in life so that his death wouldn't be seen as a sad event.

So that I may drift away with fallen petals
To a land that nobody knows.

He/she wishes to drift with the fallen petals (a form of life) and explore a land which he has not experienced.

Chu Hsiang
Translated by Kai-Yu Hsu

Use a table from the Word/Insert Table function

The verses of a poem can be put into a table by using the Word/Insert Table function with instructions explaining what to look for in a particular section of the poem. Here is a poem presented to students in this format, with questions directing them to particular aspects of each verse and space to respond:

Document 5

Smugglers

by Maria Lewitt

The poem	your response
We were met By brisk efficiency. Passport. Landing Permit. Vaccination. Chest X-Ray. Name. Nationality. And yes, – Anything to declare?	How is the sense of 'brisk efficiency' conveyed?
Hands shuffled, Fingers lifted, Eyes looked Scanned.	How do these lines continue the mood that has been established?
Nothing was confiscated. We were free to go. Our bodies bent Under the heavy cargo Of our past. We smuggled in Values and slanted opinions.	What cargo did they bring and how are these ideas conveyed?
We failed to declare Ever-lasting nostalgia, Memories of distant people, Already fading cities And lost sunsets.	How does the poet convey a sense of loss?
Nobody asked, nobody cared. We were left alone. And wherever we go, We leave a trail Of unsuspected contraband, Sometimes polluting, sometimes enriching Our adopted Home.	What words or phrases convey the idea that the new arrivals are ambivalent?

Annotation:
A focus on
close reading
of the text

Respond with graphics

Most of our contemporary poetry books have drawings or pictures, where the editor has placed his or her own pictorial interpretation of the poem as a guide for the readers. Why not let the students find their own pictures to illustrate some aspect of a poem which has appealed to them? The instruction could be:

> *Respond to this poem by selecting a word or phrase or verse. Copy the selection onto a new Word Document and illustrate your selection by choosing a picture from a web site or your clip art. Then in a few sentences, say how the words and picture complement each other.*

The rubric for a Year 9 assessment task across the classes for a poem that they had previously read and selected was:

> *Choose several lines or a phrase or key words or a series of words that were particularly vivid to you as you read the poem.*
>
> *Copy and paste these words into the next part of your response document.*
>
> *Now find on the internet or from your clip art one or two pictures, or create a collage which illustrates for you what you saw in your mind when you read those lines or words.*

Here is the pictorial response of one student to Bruce Dawe's poem 'War Without End', about the carnage on Australia's roads:

Document 6

The rusting junk-yards were not on our maps,

the rehab hospitals off-limits too,

we could not ever imagine that perhaps

someday our wheels and us might join the queue.

Needless to say, this is a very clear picture of a rusty junkyard. It is very messy – wheels, scraps of metal and old, out of shape cars. Was that a racing car? The picture is in black and white, although there are not any white places. It creates a dark, old and rusty atmosphere.

Close reading of Shakespeare

In another possible activity, the computer can be used for a close reading task. A group of Year 9 students were taken to a live production of *The Tempest*. Then for an oral assessment they were asked to choose and perform at least 100 lines from the play. As a written complement to that performance they were required to annotate and submit their selection with performance notes from the

professional production and from their own mini-production in the classroom. While many tended to use this exercise simply to 'translate' the Shakespearean words, others used the task to explore the ideas of the play. The students did not have a printed version of the play but worked entirely from a text downloaded from the Web. Here is one example:

Document 7

This scene is where Caliban and Stephano plan to kill Prospero. This is an important scene because Prospero is a very important man of the island and once he is dead his daughter will be theirs and so will the Island.

Caliban's plan to kill Prospero, so they can have his daughter

CALIBAN

Why, as I told thee, 'tis a custom with him,
I' th' afternoon to sleep: there thou mayst brain him,
Having first seized his books, or with a log
Batter his skull, or paunch him with a stake,
Or cut his wezand with thy knife. Remember
First to possess his books; for without them
He's but a sot, as I am, nor hath not
One spirit to command: they all do hate him
As rootedly as I. Burn but his books.
He has brave utensils,—for so he calls them—
Which when he has a house, he'll deck withal
And that most deeply to consider is
The beauty of his daughter; he himself
Calls her a nonpareil: I never saw a woman,
But only Sycorax my dam and she;
But she as far surpasseth Sycorax
As great'st does least.

85

90

95

100

This is where Caliban explains to Stephano how they should kill Prospero because once Prospero is dead Stephano can rule the Island and have his daughter.

Caliban explains that the first thing they must do is take Prospero's books because without them he is powerless with his magic and is just a normal person.

Calliban tells Stephano that they must burn all Prospero's books because he is useless without them. Stephano is looking very excited.

Calliban explains how beautiful Prospero's daughter Miranda is and how his mother Sycorax could never equal Miranda's beauty. This is important because it gives them another reason to want to kill Prospero. Calliban kicks the ground as he talks about his mother with anger.

Annotation:
A focus on
close reading
of the text

Close reading of a novel

We have also used the screen to set up a close reading exercise for Year 9 students, where they were given the text with questions in callout boxes and space to directly type in the answers. In the example below, the teacher's questions are in bold followed by the student response. We set up the size of the callout boxes according to the mark allocated to the question and length of the expected answer. Once more, it was easy to mark and demonstrated very quickly those who did and did not understand the levels of meaning in the novel.

Here is a small section of the response to Kelleher's *The Ivory Trail*:

Document 8

Sinking back into his chair, just as he might have done, I opened the book at the marker. The page before me was rough-edged and yellowed by time. It contained only five lines, beautifully inscribed, the ink so faded that I had to strain to read them:

The four roads that lead to XXX XXX XXX
I The way of Wonder
II The way of Selflessness
III The way of Faith

I stopped at that point, suddenly aware that what I'd read was a shorthand description of my three channellings so far. In Africa, Louis had learned the value of wonder, not freedom, as I'd first thought. For without a sense of wonder, he and Mbuqua would have remained in bondage: she is destined for the slave block, and Louis bonded to cruelty and his dream of wealth. Yes, I could see it now! The way of Wonder! The first of XXX XXX XXX's roads had opened my eyes as surely as it had opened Louis'.

What is the fourth road?

(1 mark)

The four roads that head to Ali Ben Gazrah. Those of wonder, selflessness, faith, and the fourth one, The Way of Innocence.

How and why did Mbuqua lose her bondage?

(2 marks)

In *The Elephant Hunter*, Mbuqua was given freedom by Louis, within the depths of the Matolo Mountains. Louis had realised the fact of justice, morals and wonder, and this caused him to provide Mbuqua, a slave whose life had been placed in his hands, the right of freedom.

>

41

Similarly, I could see that the English episode had dealt with more than straightforward love and hate. At the end, when John sank into the lake, he'd been prepared to risk his own life so his brother could die in peace. And if that wasn't XXX XXX XXX's way of Selflessness, then what was?

Explain how John had learnt selflessness? (5)

John and Richard Dudley had never had a close, loving, brotherly relationship. John was treated as not much better than a servant, while Richard, his half-brother, was destined to be heir to a royal position. When Richard sent John on a task to collect a gift for their sister, Lucy, John made an important decision that would affect the rest of his life. Instead of collecting the unworthy bauble, which Richard had bought for Lucy, John, disgusted by the ugliness of the object, decided to exchange it for a beautiful carving, that of the Ivory Elephant. On returning to Richard, John had presented Lucy with the gift. She had been delighted and pleased with the carving, while, Richard, on the other hand, had loathed the gift. Richard disposed of the carving, and shortly after, on his death-bed, he decided that the ivory carving held his soul. John decided that he would rescue the carving from the lake, and would not allow Richard's soul to rest on the bottom of the icy lake. In doing so, he risked his own life, for that of a brother, a brother who had never really accepted him until the last moment.

Annotation:
A focus on
close reading
of the text

Responding to newspaper issues

There is a sense of immediacy when dealing with today's news issues in the classroom. Hopefully students can learn to look beyond the simplistic 30-second TV news grab, moving on to probe current topics through editorials, opinion articles and reader's comments. Here is one example from a Year 11 student, completed in about 30 minutes:

Document 9

And now for something completely different …

By Terry Jones

For some time now, I've been trying to find out where my son goes after choir practice. He simply refuses to tell me. He says it's no business of mine where he goes after choir practice and it's a free country.

Now it may be a free country, but if people start going just anywhere they like after choir practice, goodness knows whether we'll have a country left to be free. I mean, he might be going to anarchist meetings or Islamic study groups. How do I know?

How does the writer catch the attention of the reader?
The writer catches the attention of the reader by mentioning a family member and how they worry about them. As everyone has someone special in their life, it catches their attention as the author is curious and probably worried about their special family member and the reader may have strategies to solve the situation.

In what ways is the contention of the piece being foreshadowed?
The contention of the piece is being foreshadowed by the author suggesting his son may be going to anarchist meetings or Islamic study groups.

>

The thing is, if people don't say where they're going after choir practice, this country is at risk. So I have been applying a certain amount of pressure on my son to tell me where he's going. To begin with, I simply put a bag over his head and chained him to a radiator. But did that persuade him? Does the Pope eat kosher?

My wife had the gall to suggest that I might be going a bit too far. So I put a bag over her head and chained her to the radiator. But I still couldn't persuade my son to tell me where he goes after choir practice.

I tried starving him, serving him only cold meals and shaving his facial hair off, keeping him in stress positions, not turning his light off, playing loud music outside his cell door – all the usual stuff that any concerned parent will do to find out where their child is going after choir practice. But it was all to no avail.

I hesitated to gravitate to harsher interrogation methods because, after all, he is my son. Then Donald Rumsfeld came to my rescue.

I read in *The New York Times* last week that a memo had been prepared for the US Defence Secretary on March 6, 2003. It laid down the strictest guidelines as to what is and what is not torture. Because, let's face it, none of us want to actually torture our children, in case the police get to hear about it.

Are there examples of hyperbole or exaggeration in this paragraph? If so, what is the writer trying to achieve by using them?

There are two examples of exaggeration in this paragraph: 'if people don't say where they're going after choir practice, this country is at risk' and 'To begin with, I simply put a bag over his head and chained him to a radiator'. The writer is trying to entice the reader to keep further reading and to keep them interested. He also uses the exaggeration to further emblemish his point of being worried about his son.

How is a change of tone achieved at this point in the piece and what effect does this have on the reader?

A change of tone is achieved at this point of the piece by speaking in a past tense of what he read last week. Also mentioning 'Then Donald Rumsfeld came to my rescue' further emphasied the tone. The effect that this has on the reader is that it makes the reader feel sarcasm as they realise that the author is having a shot at the US and their polices on torture of Iraq prisoners. There is a flippant tone in this section of the piece.

>

Annotation:
A focus on
close reading
of the text

Document 9 cont'd

The March 6 memo prepared for Mr Rumsfeld explained that what may look like torture is not really torture at all. It states that: if someone 'knows that severe pain will result from his actions, if causing such harm is not his objective, he lacks the requisite specific intent even though the defendant did not act in good faith'.
What this means in understandable English is that if a parent, in his anxiety to know where his son goes after choir practice, does something that will cause severe pain to his son, it is only 'torture' if the causing of that severe pain is his objective. If his objective is something else – such as finding out where his son goes after choir practice – then it is not torture.

Mr Rumsfeld's memo goes on: 'a defendant' (by which he means a concerned parent) 'is guilty of torture only if he acts with the express purpose of inflicting severe pain or suffering on a person within his control'.

Couldn't be clearer. If your intention is to extract information, you cannot be accused of torture. In fact, the report went further. It said, if a parent 'has a good-faith belief (that) his actions will not result in prolonged mental harm, he lacks the mental state necessary for his actions to constitute torture'. So all you've got to do to avoid accusations of child abuse is to say that you didn't think it would cause any lasting harm to the child. Easy peasy!

Is the writer's interpretation of Mr Rumsfeld accurate and was it necessary to paraphrase in this way?
The writer's interpretation of Mr Rumsfeld was accurate. It was necessary to paraphrase this way as it further emphasised how badly the Iraqi prisoners had been treated by US soldiers and put it into perspective for most people who in this situation would affect most people.

>

45

Document 9 cont'd

I currently have a lot of my son's friends locked up in the garage, and I'm applying electrical charges to their genitals and sexually humiliating them in order to get them to tell me where my son goes after choir practice.

Dick Cheney's counsel, David S. Addington, says that's just fine. William J. Haynes, the US Defence Department's general counsel, agrees it's just fine. And so does the US Air Force general counsel, Mary Walker.

In fact, practically everybody in the US Administration seems to think it's just fine, except for the State Department lawyer, William H. Taft IV, who perversely claims that I might be opening the door to people applying electrical charges to my genitals and sexually humiliating me.

So I'm going to round up all the children in the neighbourhood, chain them and set dogs on them. I might accidentally kill one or two – but I won't have intended to – and perhaps I'll take some photos of my wife standing on the dead bodies, and then I'll show the photos to the other kids, and finally, perhaps, I might get to find out where my son goes after choir practice.

After all, I'll only be doing what the US Administration has been condoning since September 11.

Terry Jones (www.terry-jones.net) is a writer, film director, actor and Python. This article first appeared in The Guardian. *Re-published in* The Age, *19 June 2004.*

Are there any examples of sarcasm or other devices of persuasion? If so, how do they contribute to the argument?
There are a couple examples of sarcasm. One example is 'I currently have a lot of my son's friends locked up in the garage, and I'm applying electrical charges to their genitals and sexually humiliating them in order to get them to tell me where my son goes after choir practice'. They contribute to the argument as if this was happening to people's children, it would no way near be accepted as much as the Iraq situation. The sarcasm contributes greatly, as it influences people to accept his argument.

Summarise the writer's contention. How effective do you find this as a piece of persuasive writing?
The writer's contention is that the actions of the US Administration in Iraq with dealing with prisoners should be condemned and should not be condoned or approved of because 'they may be a terrorist'. This piece of writing is effective, but at the start of the piece it was hard to follow. The clear contention only comes clear after the mention of Donald Rumsfeld, but until then I found it a bit awkward. I did though think it was clever and a very confronting and persuasive piece of writing.

Annotation:
A focus on
close reading
of the text

Annotation of cartoons

Being able to discern and articulate the elements in a cartoon is an important skill for students to learn. The rubric for such a task could be:

This cartoon below appeared in 2003 in an Iranian newspaper (soon after the declared end of the second Gulf War).

Use at least three callout boxes to annotate it.

Point out significant details and explain what the message or contention of the cartoonist is.

Here is a response by a Year 11 student, completed in class in a limited time:

Document 10

WTF?

America. Looting Iraq, passing down the pieces to Israel. On top of the world. World POLICE.

Israel is portrayed to be malevolent and scoring from the war with Iraq: oil, favouritism from UN, OPEC. From Iran's point of view, Israel are crooks.

CARTOONISTS & WRITERS SYNDICATE http://CartoonWeb.com

MEHDI KEYHAN
TEHRAN
IRAN

Snake = Tony Blair. Backup for USA. Hoping to 'score' from aftermath of war.

This Year 11 student has not managed to get all the details right in the cartoon, but has made a reasonable attempt to understand an Arab perspective on a current and controversial topic. He has not seen the significance of the tree and snake in the Garden of Eden, and Africa is not the WTF, but for all that, we had a good starting point for discussion when his and other responses were put up on screen with a data projector.

Wider applications and suggested activities

Comparison of newspaper coverage

The immediacy of this kind of teaching can be really exhilarating. Find a topical issue and see how it is dealt with in more than one newspaper. For example, you could compare the reporting of a world event in a local newspaper with the report in a Singapore or Shanghai or Berlin newspaper.

Use the National Library web site http://www.nla.gov.au/npapers/

Or the Web addresses of all Australian newspapers: http://www.start4all.com/ newspapers/aus.htm

Or http://www.newspapers.com/ for newspapers overseas OR use a search engine to find your own.

Or the Internet Public Library for every newspaper online from around the world http://www.ipl.org/div/news/

Get students started by asking them to copy this table into a new document, then paste in the articles:

News topic:	
Australian Newspaper:	Overseas Newspaper:
Writer:	Writer:
Date:	Date:
The Article	The Article
My comments	My comments

Teaching history research methods

Often in the middle years students study the history of their own school as a way of establishing good methodology for the subject. They could do this by studying the periods that each headmaster served or key events, building developments or other points of significance.[8]

Using the Microsoft Word/Drawing Toolbar/AutoShapes/Connectors and Lines students could tackle the following:

- *Start with the foundation date of the school*
- *Add some key dates like the ones below using callouts. (Go to the Drawing Toolbar/AutoShapes/ Callouts.)*

Annotation:
A focus on
close reading
of the text

- *Add 1907 – First magazine published*
- *Add 1917 – House system established*
- *Add 1926 – Junior School built*
- *Add 1953 – P and F Hall built*
- *Add 1973 – Science wing started*
- *Add 1980 – Swimming pool built*
- *Add 1992 – First interschool athletics premiership*
- *2003 – Centenary*
- *When you started at the school*
- *ADD at least three illustrations or decorations. Use the school's web if you wish.*

Annotation in geography

In a geography class, students could be asked to annotate an Editorial or Letter to the Editor about the siting of a toxic waste dump. They would examine the text by asking: 'What is being said?' 'Who is saying it and why?' and 'What position are they coming from – is it simply a "Not in My Back Yard" argument?'

It is immediately clear that these concepts and skills are common across many subjects and offer a challenge to a narrow view of subject disciplines.

Endnotes

[1] J. McKenzie, *How teachers learn technology best*, FNO Press, 1999, p. 79.

[2] R. Andrews, 'Framing and design in ICT in English: towards a new subject and new practices in the classroom', in A. Goodwyn (ed.), *English in the digital age: information and communications technology and the teaching of English*, Cassell, London, 2000, p. 27.

[3] A. Goodwyn (ed.), 2000, op cit, Chapter 8, 'Texting, reading and writing in the Internet', p. 128.

[4] D. McRae, 'What to make and why – principles for the design and development of online curriculum content', Summary Document, Curriculum Corporation, Australia, March 2001, p. 4.

[5] ibid., pp. 4, 5.

[6] ibid., p. 9.

[7] Reproduced here with permission of the author, John Schuman, singer/songwriter and former lead singer of the band, Redgum.

[8] Classroom activity prepared by Diane McDonald and the History teachers at Trinity Grammar School, Kew.

Chapter 5

'[Education is] about creating a kind of person able to navigate change and diversity, learn-as-they-go, solve problems, collaborate, and be flexible and creative ... promoting capability, reflexive and autonomous learning, collaboration, communication ...'[1]

Oral language:
Avoiding death by PowerPoint

The learning and thinking context

Oral language activities have been accorded a far higher status in the past few years in secondary schools.[2] These activities can include specifically planned, structured and orchestrated tasks which the teacher prepares and mediates in order to extend the oracy of the class.[3] They may also include small group learning, formal student presentations to a group or the whole class, and will certainly include an encouragement to good listening. It is fundamental that the 'classroom teacher and students alike must assume that students have something to learn from each other'. It is not necessary for the 'teacher to be the keeper and controller of the "talking space"'.[4]

In *Re-Viewing English*, a significant 1998 text for Australian English teachers, the role of the teacher in engendering the optimal learning environment for oracy is summed up as:

Plan, prepare, orchestrate and mediate meaningful and enjoyable language experiences ...
Establish and affirm through practice the patterns of expectation about acceptable and unacceptable talk;
Encourage a view of discussion as a means of enlarging one's personal world view and modifying it to take account of other people's;
Have a repertoire of appropriate questioning techniques;
Act as a facilitator, co-ordinator, receptive audience, negotiator, consultant and supportive mentor ...
Intervene when necessary, challenge, redirect or refocus talk to encourage students to move beyond the mere expression of opinion ...[5]

We have all sat through tedious PowerPoint presentations where the presenter turns away from the audience and reads an essay off the screen. As an alternative, try peer assessment of presentations in small groups where three or four students sit around a computer screen; insist on 36 point type with six words per dot point and six dot points per slide; give students practice in eye-balling an audience without turning to see what is on the screen behind them.

One of the best presentations I have heard was from a Year 12 girl who delivered a passionate plea for the reintroduction of the death sentence. To complement her talk, a PowerPoint presentation ran behind her with one photograph of a victim of Timothy McVeigh's Oklahoma bombing scrolling across the screen every ten seconds. Her point was driven home very forcefully indeed. We do not have to subject ourselves or our students to 'death by PowerPoint' or 'PowerPointlessness' as Jamie McKenzie calls it.[6]

In Chapter 2, reference was made to constructivist learning theories, where the learner is an active participant in constructing knowledge. A linking of the oral language with the vast potential of computers is a great way to put this theory into practice.

Classroom strategies

The following are some ideas for learning activities through formal and informal oral work in order to achieve sound learning outcomes.

A single PowerPoint slide as an aid to an oral presentation

Here is a rubric for an oral presentation which was used with a Year 11 class after they had studied an anthology of short stories in a traditional way:

Choose ONE sentence from a story that is different to the one you will use for the succeeding tasks.

Find ONE picture or drawing that for you illustrates that sentence or assists your understanding of the scene.

Present the text and the illustration in ONE PowerPoint slide.

Use that slide as a basis for the explanation of what you found significant in the story, or the way the writer expressed the details or any other aspect that you found notable.

Be prepared to read aloud to the class a section of the story. The reading and your explanation should take between two and three minutes.

For more details of the rubric, see Chapter 11.

One student used the very simple slide opposite to talk about the story 'The Road to Rankin's Point' from the collection *The Lost Salt Gift of Blood*. Using this single slide as a focus, he pointed out the timeframe of the story, the age of the grandmother and the harsh life she had led, the voice of the narrator grandson and the major events of the story. It was brilliantly simple and effective.

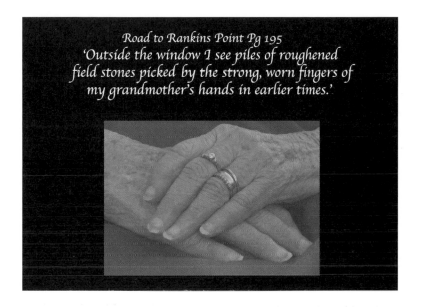

PowerPoint for formal assessment

A Year 8 class, studying the novel *Songman* by Alan Baillie, was given the following task with very specific instructions about the number of slides and the number of words to be used, with the following rubric:

- *Prepare a PowerPoint presentation of six slides.*
- *The presentation must include some graphics and/or sound clips.*

- *A maximum of six dot points and a maximum of six words per dot point.*
- *Using the Notes Page View, each slide must be accompanied by about 50 words of explanation.*

The presentation was to take no longer than ten minutes and be delivered to a group of three or four around a computer screen in a lab. The presentation was then peer-assessed according to the following criteria, although the teacher reserved the right to allocate the final mark using the student assessment and observations while moving around from group to group:

PEER ASSESSMENT of the PRESENTATION	5	4	3	2	1	0
Involved the audience (eye contact, answered questions, etc)						
Structure of the slides (coherence and development of ideas)						
Expressiveness (control of features of spoken English)						
Knowledge of content (effective exploration of the book, evidence of research, etc)						
Comments:						

In addition, the students were required to prepare a 50-word summary for each slide in 'speaker's notes', and then print the slide and the notes using the PowerPoint/Print/Notes pages to submit for teacher assessment. Here is a slide prepared by one girl:

Yukuwa's Tribe

- Love eating yams, apples, wallabies
- Collect and hunt own food from the land
- Skin is black
- Believe in superstitions
- Moved from beach to beach
- Wife cannot abandon injured husband

The notes which she printed for this page (with uncorrected syntax) were:

Yolngu is another name for Yukuwa's tribe. Their skin is very black because they live under the high sun. They never stayed in one place like the Macassans – they always moved from beach to beach. It's part of their culture. The Yolngu people collect their own food from the land. They believe that the land provided them food. So they never plant their food like the Macassans. Yolngu people love eating yam, apples, and duck eggs which the women and children would find plus wallabies, crocodile, kangaroo which the men would hunt for, then they would have a feast. The Yolngu people have strong superstition. They believe that if you disturbed a dead person's grave, the spirit, the galka, can causes trouble for the tribe and bring bad luck like One Eye Grave post. It is the Yolngu Law that if a wife deserted her injured husband, the women must die.

The criteria for the assessment of the written part of the task were:

	Max	Mark awarded
Knowledge of content and exploration of ideas	12	
Coherence and effective organisation, paragraphing, and relevance to the slide.	4	
Control of the mechanics of language, spelling, etc	4	
Total	20	
Comment:		

Using PowerPoint to present a 'choose your own adventure' story

Students find it quite easy to set up hyperlinks within a PowerPoint story and then enjoy teasing their peers with the directions the story may take. Here is the slide from a Year 8 piece of creative writing where the audience, which listens to the story being read to them, chooses which way they want to take the story:

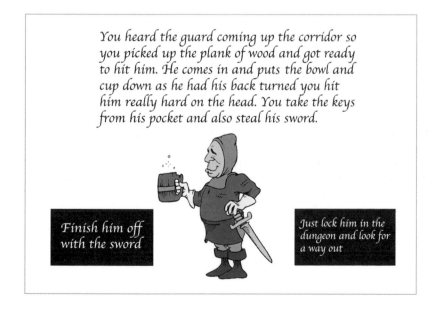

You heard the guard coming up the corridor so you picked up the plank of wood and got ready to hit him. He comes in and puts the bowl and cup down as he had his back turned you hit him really hard on the head. You take the keys from his pocket and also steal his sword.

Finish him off with the sword

Just lock him in the dungeon and look for a way out

In similar fashion, students in a Year 8 Religion and Society class used the same facility in PowerPoint to chart a path through the temptations of marijuana:

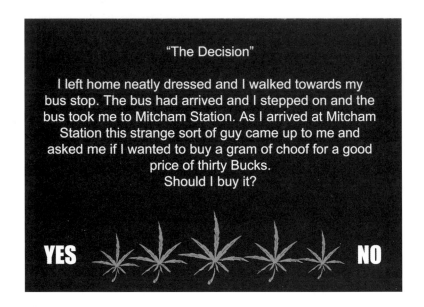

Using an Excel graph to promote class discussion

A teacher working with a senior secondary class that was nearing the end of reading and studying *Hamlet*, took a straw poll on what the students considered to be the factors which led to the multiple tragedies in the last act of the play. Students were given two votes each and the data was quickly entered in a Microsoft Excel spreadsheet:

Factors contributing to the final tragedy in *Hamlet*	
Gertrude's quick new marriage	2
Hamlet's madness	15
Laertes' desire for revenge	7
Claudius' ambition to be king	10
Procrastination by Hamlet	17
Doubt that the ghost could be trusted	4
Weakness of women	6
Polonius spying on his daughter	1
Rotten political structures in Denmark	3

From there it was a matter of a few seconds to translate that data into a graph:

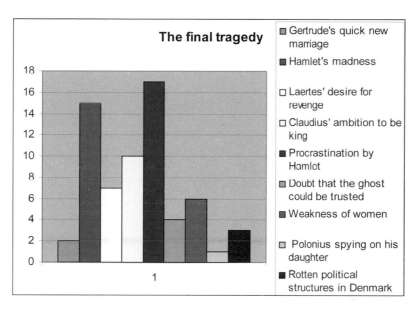

Vigorous discussion ensued when the graph was projected onto a screen. Those who voted for the weakness of women were challenged, as were those wanting to wipe their hands of the whole thing by saying that Hamlet was mad. It was a good way of pushing students beyond quick and easy answers.

Use of organisational charts to summarise group discussion

Something visual can focus the attention of students and provoke discussion. Word XP has an easy-to-use diagram gallery in the Drawing Toolbar. For example, a group could utilise the organisational chart to explore the consequences of anti-communist paranoia in Australia in the late 1940s:

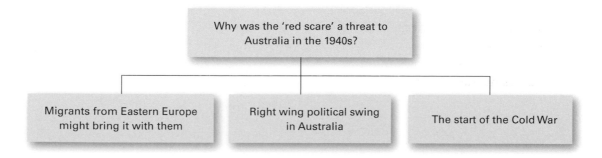

This is no more than a quick five-minute classroom exercise that encourages students to think, talk and tease out ideas. The very fact that groups of students can approach a topic in quite different ways and then have to defend their position sharpens their critical perspective. The visual representation on a computer for a group or via a data projector for a class is simply a way of focusing their thinking. Chalk, paper and crayons would do just as well but are more cumbersome and time-consuming.

Another template from the organisational chart is the cycle diagram, which could be used to plot the consequences of land degradation:

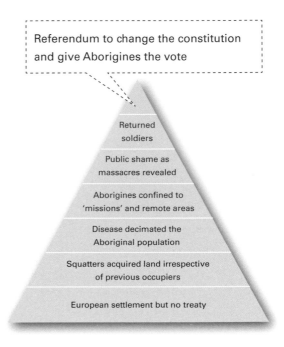

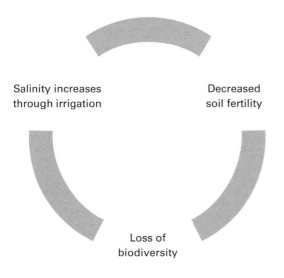

Alternatively, students could use a pyramid chart to plot the steps that led to the granting of citizenship to Aborigines in Australia in 1967.

A Venn diagram could be used to make a diagrammatic representation of the common interests of Laertes, Gertrude and Polonius, such as:

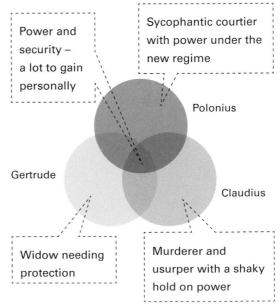

There are a total of six different charts in the diagram gallery but many students will probably prefer to construct their own from the AutoShapes/Flowchart patterns in Word or with an Inspiration map.

Students revising Hamlet were put into random pairs to tease out concepts from the play, such as power, revenge, trust, greed, fear, friendship and others, which they could choose from a list. They were then given 30 minutes to tease out the concept, find supporting evidence from at least three scenes and summarise their understanding on poster paper or with an Inspiration map. All then presented their conclusions to the class within the same lesson. Here is the diagram screened by one pair via the data projector to support their explanation:

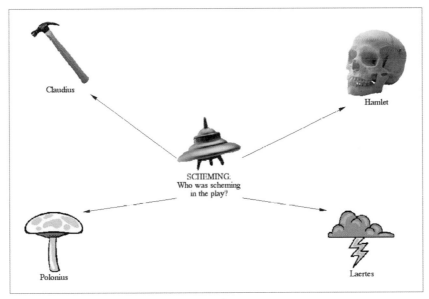

Diagram created in Inspiration® by Inspiration Software®, Inc.

Their brief notes on Claudius were:

Claudius' fear of Hamlet resulted in him plotting to get rid of Hamlet after his 'play within a play' set-up. He first decides to send him to England in Act III, Scene I (a reversal on his original plan to keep him under close watch), but then upgrades the plan in Act IV, Scene III to have him murdered in England.

Hamlet escapes the fate designed for him and returns. The King then takes advantage of Laertes' anger, convincing him that Hamlet is to blame for the deaths of his sister and father.

Claudius also plots when he pays Rozencrantz and Guildenstern to watch Hamlet and pose as his friends.

A poetry example – defending the indefensible

In a Year 11 study of the poetry of TS Eliot, students were asked to select what they saw as key lines and present them to the class with a picture which complemented the ideas of the poem. It was a simple homework exercise which then took only 15 minutes the following day for all the students to present on screen. The purpose was merely to encourage students to look closely at the text for themselves and read aloud that part of the poem to the class with some explanation. One boy produced the following:

His slide produced a hostile reaction from the class. Not one of his peers agreed that the image was consistent with the intention of the poet and he had to struggle very hard to explain why he had chosen it. The following example was far easier to defend:

It was a quick and interesting exercise that produced the valuable 'teachable moment' and forced the students to look carefully at the poem. None chose the same lines to discuss so it turned out to be a good summary exercise as well.

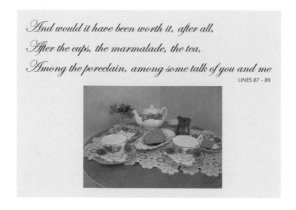

Wider applications
and suggested activities

Computers offer exciting challenges for teachers and present students with stimulating ways for thinking and responding.

Most schools have data projectors which can be booked and are easily accessible to teachers. Despite the frustrations that this may involve, the more they are booked and used, the more pressure it will place on the administrators to buy more.

Ideally there should be one projector per room, but oral does not have to be a whole-class experience. We have often split a class in half for oral work when there has been a student teacher to take some of the class to the next room. In most schools the librarians, and sometimes colleagues, are willing to assist with this kind of assessment activity. It is necessary, however, to train students to work in groups, and to assess each other in these groups. Students tend to bunch the marks, being reluctant to give very high or very low scores, but

the rank order is usually spot on and the comments often mean more coming from a fellow student than they would from the teacher.

Peer evaluation of an oral book report

Wide reading is an individual activity but it must also be accountable in some way. Written book reports are boring to write and read or may have been plagiarised from the http://www.amazon.com web site. On the other hand, an oral presentation where a student can show the book to peers and read some sections can be very stimulating and encourage an awareness of new genres and authors. Web research may give some wider background to the novelist, plot or setting. Overleaf is the assessment sheet we have used for this activity with instructions to group leaders and a requirement that talks be timed:

Peer evaluation of an oral book report

Name of presenter _____

Title of the book _____   Author _____

Time: (4–6 minutes)	VH	H	M	L	NS
The presenter has recently read the whole book.					
The presenter had a good understanding of the plot and characters.					
The presenter read aloud an appropriate passage and explained the context.					
The talk was well prepared with an obvious structure and correct time.					
The presenter communicated well, had a clear voice, made good eye contact with the audience and did *not* read a script.					

Comments and suggestions for improvement _____

_____

Name of evaluator _____   Date _____

This task could be adapted to any subject and there are more suggestions about book reports in one of the models in Chapter 11.

Planning a three-day excursion

A Year 6 class about to go on a three-day excursion to the national capital spent a lesson sitting on the floor in groups with their wireless-enabled laptops, each group searching a different place or activity that they might be visiting or engaged in on the trip. Each student in the group searched different resources related to their topic. After allowing

time for searching, they were given 15 minutes for each group to prepare a PowerPoint summary of what they had just discovered. For the final part of the lesson, the teacher brought in a data projector and each group shared what they had learnt with the class.

Summarising arguments for a debate

This idea of oral assessment can be just as easily applied to a 'Power and Politics' topic in middle school or an economics topic in senior school. A group in a middle school class could, for example,

Oral language:
Avoiding death
by PowerPoint

be asked to discuss a topic such as 'Does Australia have enough water for us to be growing cotton at all?', while another group could deal with the consequences of controlling the flow of our river systems. Each group could summarise their considerations in an Excel graph, as suggested above, or summarise their main points in a PowerPoint slide and show these on a screen for all the class to see and debate. This is a basic classroom technique which is effective across many subjects but one that computers help to facilitate. Students enjoy the challenge of justifying their opinions to their peers, just as the peers no doubt enjoy challenging the assumptions that a group has made.

Endnotes

[1] Australian Council of the Deans of Education, *New learning: a charter for Australian education*, ACDE, 2001, Proposition 4.

[2] In Victoria, oral work is now a component of the School Assessed Course work (SAC) which accounts for 50 per cent of the final tertiary entrance grade in English. As we might expect, higher level assessment inevitably drives curriculum innovation in lower grades.

[3] The revised New South Wales curriculum document, currently in the process of implementation, includes a requirement for students in the middle secondary years to be able to 'express considered points of view in speech or writing, accurately and coherently and with confidence and fluency in rehearsed, unrehearsed and impromptu situations.' For this and more details see <http://www.boardofstudies.nsw.edu.au/syllabus_sc/pdf_doc/english_710_syllabus.pdf> viewed 27 April 2004.

[4] W. Sawyer, K. Watson & E. Gold (eds), *Re-viewing English*, St Clair Press, Sydney, 1998, pp. 268–9.

[5] ibid., p. 269.

[6] J. McKenzie, 'We've done the Internet. Now what?' Speech presented at a seminar in Melbourne, 28 February 2004.

Chapter 6

'I am looking for creative, adaptable professionals with an interest in and capacity to learn and the ability to be a role model for this in their classrooms.'[1]

Online discussion:

A challenge for thinking skills

The learning and thinking context

The driving force for the 'Philosophy in Schools' movement, where the classroom is thought of as a community of enquiry, comes out of the work of Ann Sharp in the United States, Lawrence Splitter in Australia and others. 'Dialogue lies at the heart of all enquiry', says Splitter, 'be it within the context of specific disciplines like history, philosophy and mathematics or within the broader framework of social and world problems'. This may range 'from engaging in dialogue and asking probing questions to a preparedness to correct one's thinking and treat other persons' work with care'.[2]

All teachers would love to think that their classrooms are places where opinions are respected and a range of viewpoints can be canvassed and scrutinised. This seems even more necessary in the face of bland, conforming stereotypes that are 'fed to us by much of today's media and the mindlessness of music videos and anti-intellectualism which seems to bombard us all'.[3] We are often fed 30-second news grabs and one-dimensional opinions in the popular press, so it is more vital than ever that all teachers encourage students to think critically about assumptions, beliefs and values.

The 'New Basics' curriculum project in Queensland contains the following statement about higher order thinking skills across every subject:

Higher-order thinking requires students to manipulate information and ideas in ways that transform their meaning and implications. This transformation occurs when students combine facts and ideas in order to synthesise, generalise, explain, hypothesise or arrive at some conclusion or interpretation. Manipulating information and ideas through these processes allows students to solve problems and discover new (for them) meanings and understandings. When students engage in the construction of knowledge, an element of uncertainty is introduced into the instructional process and makes instructional outcomes not always predictable ... In helping students become producers of knowledge, the teacher's main instructional task is to create activities or environments that allow them opportunities to engage in higher-order thinking.[4]

Contrary to popular myth, computers do not need to be isolating instruments where the supposed 'nerdy' students put their heads in the screen and let the rest of the world go by! Ideally we would like to see a collaborative learning community where participants are brought together to address issues or solve problems in a secure, supportive environment. Schneiderman, in his challenging book *Leonardo's Laptop*, envisages

> *computer rich networked classrooms [which] make possible a variety of collaborations. Students can create on their computers and show the whole class for discussion with a large-screen projector or by copying to every student's computer. By rapidly reviewing student work, everyone can see the range of good to bad work and sharpen their reviewing skills. With appropriate software, classroom brainstorming among dozens of students can, within minutes, produce an amazing variety of comments … and encourage diverse and creative suggestions.[5]*

One of the best ways of getting students to focus away from themselves may be to persuade them to engage mentally with someone outside their normal peer group orbit. A constructivist educator will encourage students to test their understandings, engage in dialogue with the teacher and one another, and ask thoughtful, open-ended questions of each other.[6] Surely ICT provides a powerful new medium for this kind of interaction.

One teacher in Essex, UK, says that her students found the Web

> *a powerful, new and effective way of communicating with others. Given that speaking and listening skills are, for most of us, our most used and most important methods of communication, I was heartened by the way in which these students embraced and celebrated their membership of the chat world.[7]*

Researchers have found that girls tend to dominate linguistic space in a classroom, while boys are less inclined than girls to engage in talk as a means of exploring their ideas. In one study, boys did demonstrate their enjoyment in participating in small-group literature discussions but this depended on the socio-cultural factors of what constitutes a good discussion, the teacher's control of strategies that supported dialogue, and a classroom pedagogy that embraced collaborative inquiry.[8]

In the following examples from classroom practice, the group of teachers involved had not abandoned face-to-face class and group discussion, but rather complemented these by using the very flexible digital tools now so readily available to us.

Classroom **strategies**

Senior English text discussion online

Chat rooms are a familiar milieu for students and are a mode of communication where abbreviations and trivial comments are the accepted norm. But just as schoolyard or changeroom chatter is not acceptable in style or format for a formal piece of written work or a classroom oral presentation, so the conventions of student-to-student chat rooms are not acceptable in a structured academic discussion.

A group of colleagues decided to test some assumptions about online discussion for educative purposes by setting up Web-based chat groups across eight Year 11 English classes. A researcher, who viewed the process from an external perspective, concluded that students were able to carry out group discussion in an educationally sound way and look at various levels of meaning in a text as they formulated and re-formulated their thinking. The majority of students, she said, were able to engage in scholarly dialogue with someone outside their normal social group. Shyer students, ESL students and those who valued opportunities for more reflective debate appeared in particular to prefer online discussions to face-to-face discussions of the class text. Of course, classroom interactions continued, but this online environment catered in a different way for students with specific personality and learning styles.[9]

In this scenario, one student from each of the Year 11 English classes was randomly allocated to a group of seven or eight students. Each teacher from across the eight classes scaffolded the discussion and moderated several groups, with students not necessarily from their own classes. As there were over 200 students in that year level, many did not know each other, so there had to be genuine communication outside the normal peer group. An electronic record was kept of what each student wrote. Each teacher/moderator was asked to intervene from time to time in the discussion and evaluate the frequency and quality of the student responses to the text *In the Lake of the Woods* by Tim O'Brien, noting particularly how students followed and contributed to a discussion, presented evidence, and respected and responded to the views of others.

The specific goals for this task were defined as:

- Encourage students to engage in a reflective and thinking activity with someone outside their class, normal friendship group or normal comfort zone.
- Carry out a group discussion in a way that would be educationally sound but more difficult in a direct face-to-face way.
- Provide a basis for further oral responses as students look at the various levels of meaning in the text.

- Give students an opportunity to interact with an English teacher other than their own and so enrich and broaden their learning experience.

- Experiment with the technology to ensure that we can use this method for further online discussion at other year levels and between schools.

Here is a small sample of the discussion from one group:

Teacher/Moderator:
Before he realises Kathy is missing, John decides to get his life in order. Isn't this a sign that he felt he could move on and find something approaching happiness? Are we trapped by our past? Could Wade have made a new life for himself that didn't involve deceit?

Ron (responding to one early contribution):
Well Carmen, I happen to disagree with this statement of yours. Firstly John was definitely a prisoner of his past. His father's death was out of his control and caused him to feel angry and at times have outbursts of anger. Due to his past John was not a good soldier because he did not possess the qualities that a 'Good Soldier' should have. He was self-centred and scared. He only wanted to go to war to build on his political status. His whole life, John was in a desperate search for love, power and control. His political failure after the war and his diminishing marriage with Kathy shows us that he was indeed a prisoner of a past that left him alone and desperate for love.

Fiona:
It would have been better had Wade come clean about his past the moment he thought about running for the US Senate, not so much that he was involved in the My Lai massacre, but more that he tried to 'cover his tracks' by rewriting official military files. If Wade did reveal all this, Kathy would probably have stayed with him, but his political career would be ended. People would simply not want someone who had done so much lying to represent them in the Government.

Carmen:
Yes – this may be true – that John decides to get his life back into order before he realises Kathy is missing, but it does show he can move on and approach happiness. This would have been Wade's theory when starting out in the political world – move on, forget Vietnam and find happiness. As we can see this did not work, and it did not help him 'move on' as we can see that a large portion of himself did not move on from Vietnam or his childhood.

This is a perfect example of how our past is with us always. When we do something wrong, when we make a mistake, people comfort us by saying 'don't worry, the past is the past – it is forgotten about', and these sort of comments make us feel better. John probably thought this after the whole Vietnam saga: 'forget about it, start a new life and let the past fade away'. In the instance of Wade making a new life, well in Wade's case it couldn't be done because he had no one he could really turn to. Yes – he did love Kathy – but he could not confide in her, and tell her his secrets. If there is no one in your life you can really trust then it is extremely hard to create a new person – as you yourself begin to forget who you were, and therefore you lose a sense of purpose and reality. John's life didn't really involve deceit – it was not purposeful or intentional the bad things that he did. It was the way he went about covering them up that was deceitful.

>

Carmen:
Sorry Ron – I see what you mean by me not answering the question properly – I actually meant it to answer the other question – that he was trapped by his past. So if you could bear this in mind, and re-read the question, my answer may make a bit more sense. SORRY!

Teacher:
Ron, surely Wade was a successful soldier – he was promoted and received commendations. What definition are you using to support your argument?

Fiona:
Is there such a thing as a good soldier?

Ron:
We need more topics!!!!

Middle school discussion as an extension activity

A discussion was similarly set up for an extension group of Year 7 students who read the novel *Hitler's Daughter* by Jackie French outside their normal English curriculum. A very simple but password-protected discussion was set up in Microsoft Outlook for the group of 20 students who were selected from five different classes but who rarely met together physically.

We started one thread by asking the students to define genocide and reflect on current examples in Rwanda, Kurdistan, The Sudan, East Timor and other places. We also asked if they thought it was appropriate for 12-year-old students to be discussing this topic. One student responded quickly to this challenge by referring to the genocide of Australian Aborigines then said,

The theme of genocide should be discussed in Year 7 because I think that when people reach Year 7, they sort of start to want to know about things that are happening outside of their little part of the world.

The next student picked up the argument immediately with, 'I don't agree with Steven. Oh by the way I am Melanie.'

The following student started with, 'Hi this is Ying here', and continued with a surprisingly mature comment,

In my mind genocide occurs when one religious group wants to get rid of the other such as the Serbs and the Kosovars. Another time we hear about genocide is when a country wants to get rid of people in another country, for example, the Indonesians in West Papua New Guinea. A final example would be where a dictator and his military wants to get rid of a race such as in Iraq where the dictator Saddam Hussein killed millions of Iraq people and Pinochet murdered millions of his own people in Argentina.

Then a student, who had previously not joined in, clearly felt so comfortable with the group that she was prepared to make a very personal contribution. She wrote,

> Hey guys. I'm Agnes.
>
> I find Genocide particularly disgusting, as my family were involved in the Holocaust. My father's parents parents were Jews, and were living in Germany and Austria at the time. They were taken into camps, and my great grandfather died very early on. However, my great grandmother lived through seven long years of torture. I think people find genocide particularly horrible when they have been through it. They know what it is like to be hated for no reason, and killed for no reason. Although we all know that it is horrible, I believe that we don't really know what it is like.

The teacher then tried to bring the discussion back to the novel by asking students to reflect on war guilt and why German people appeared to follow Hitler so blindly. This is part of Dimitri's response:

> Can we blame Hitler for what he did? Or would he be able to realise what is wrong and right? I think German families would have gone on family outings, like picnics, just like us. It says in the book, when Fraulein Mundt is talking to Heidi, that the people of Germany (most of them) looked up to Hitler because he wanted to give them more jobs and a new name for Germany, after the First World War. Hitler promised this, nobody else did and people wanted him to win. So for a while the Germans probably went along with him, almost being sort of hypnotised. Probably after a few months they began to realise what he was doing was evil. Imagine the faith they must have held in Hitler . . . .

In the course of various discussions, we observed that students who have ideas but are slow thinkers, finding it difficult to get their ideas together quickly in a face-to-face discussion, find this a supportive and less confronting medium. Similarly, ESL students, who often like taking their time to compose at the keyboard, said that they enjoyed the discussions more than on-the-spot comments in class. It is easy for both these groups to be intimidated in a classroom by the extroverts or the quick thinkers.

Talented students are another group who appear well suited to online discussion. They have lots of ideas and enjoy a meeting of minds but often can't be bothered saying much in a mixed ability class where they can be easily put down or ignored. Sitting in front of a screen is more private, even in a classroom, although this can also be done at home or for that matter, anywhere else in the world. One of our students continued her contributions while on a short study exchange in Europe.

Discussion across the world – the classroom without walls

We invited a group of Year 10 students, who had been selected by their teachers as talented writers, to participate in an extension activity by joining in an online discussion. They were clearly enthusiastic and motivated students, although not all accepted the invitation. We also invited students from a school in California and one in South Africa to join in.[10] We had no illusions that a first experiment of this kind would produce much serious or reflective thinking, but it was a start and it was at least useful for the teachers to see the pitfalls in this potentially positive learning situation.

Our first topic was 'Terrorism affects overseas travel'. While 107 students viewed the topic there were only two brief replies. Clearly this did not grab the interest of the students despite its very topical nature.

The second topic 'Why do Australians, who generally don't favour capital punishment, want the death penalty for the Bali bombers?' was read 67 times but drew only five brief replies. Again this was a surprising deadend because it was a topic that carried a very high profile, at least in the Australian media, at the time.

One student from South Africa, started a new thread 'The US led war in Iraq was wrong'. This was looked at 13 times but provoked no reaction at all.

A student then started a vitriolic topic: 'The US contains the most morons in the world', and this became an unproductive slanging match, probably between two students in the same school but as the free discussion board we chose to use was not password protected, there was no way of knowing which school the students came from. Previous experience had shown that 15-year-old students found it a bit babyish to introduce themselves and their school so this time we had tried to get quickly into some discussion.

Clearly the topic which sparked the most interest was 'The treatment of the US President in the Australian Parliament', following the visit by George Bush to Canberra in October 2003 to thank Australians for their participation in the second Gulf war.

This message was viewed 345 times and there were 18 replies. Two boys from the Australian school, one with a conservative perspective and one with a strong leftwing opinion, started off the discussion which obviously then offended some of the American students, but got surprising support from some whom we presumed were South Africans.

This was the topic the teachers initiated to generate discussion:

The scenario: last week, George Bush addressed the Australian Parliament. A Greens Senator, Bob Brown, interrupted the President and was ejected from the chamber. He questioned the fate of the two Australians being held without charge in Guantanamo Bay. The rules of Parliament here do not permit the filming of anyone except the person speaking. A CNN crew ignored these rules and filmed the interjection and eviction and that footage was then shown on US and Australian TV. Would you like to comment on one or more of these questions:

1 *Was the interruption just bad manners?*
2 *Does this just support the anti-war cause?*
3 *Should CNN have shown the footage?*
4 *Should the President have expected anti-war feeling?*
5 *The Chinese Premier Hu doing exactly the same thing the next day required the public gallery to be cleared of dissidents. Did he have the right as a guest in a foreign country to demand this?*

The following is a sample of the 18 replies.

AAAA: 'Personally I feel that Senator Bob Brown and Kerry Nettle were quite immature and irresponsible in the way they treated George Bush during his speech to Parliament. They broke the rules of Parliament and showed a complete lack of respect by interrupting the US President twice. They are allowed to disagree and hold a silent protest, but they shouldn't have heckled the man. In regards to CNN filming in Parliament during the President's speech, I feel that they shouldn't have been allowed to, however it was a major event in the Australian media at the time so the footage would have been highly sought after.'

BBBB: 'Just in response to AAAA: What Bob Brown and Kerry Nettle did was very appropriate. George Bush is just as much a terrorist as Saddam Hussein and opposing him is not immature, nor is it irresponsible. It is disgraceful that Parliament – the house of the people – was closed to protestors on this day. It was a shameful act for (Australian Prime Minister) Howard to jump on the unjustified war bandwagon and now he turns away from the people as well.'

CCCC: 'Yes, the decision to go to war so quickly (Iraq) was questionable and I personally think that if he went, he should've waited until there was rock-hard evidence. That's if he had to go to war at all. War should be the absolute last option for anybody to take and in the result, I think it may have made the American people a bit more arrogant about thinking they own Iraq and Afghanistan.'

DDDD: 'In reply to BBBB, I would like to know how you classify our President, George Bush as a terrorist in the same way as you look at Saddam Hussein. Our President has done nothing in comparison to Saddam.'

EEEE: 'My response is directed towards BBBB, why would you classify President George Bush as a terrorist? What would make you think that he's as bad as Saddam or Bin Ladin? What Bob Brown and Kerry Nettle did was very inappropriate. They should have respected President Bush by not blurting out. They should have been mature enough to wait until he was done.'

FFFF: 'Responding to BBBB. Why would you consider President Bush a terrorist? He does everything for our country to STOP terrorisms. I feel his decision to choose to go to war was a good decision. Go President Bush!!!'

GGGG: 'I agree with BBBB a little bit, but he is not as much as Osama but he is a horrible pres. Bush does not care about the environment. He attacked Iraq and they had nothing to do with 9/11. I think he cheated on the election. More on my last thing – Bush took us out of the nuclear arms act, does not believe in the ozone hole and broke treaties.'

HHHH: 'I think that anyone that has something bad to say please keep it to yourself.'

JJJJJ to HHHH: 'Don't be a bad example! Try to keep you anger inside and respect other people's opinions. If BBBB thinks he is a terrorist, let him. If you don't agree, calmly say it.'

Wider applications
and suggested activities

The above examples were a first attempt to use this new medium in the style of a Web chat room with which the students were well familiar. We knew that we were probably breaking new ground in the ways we were going about it and that we may very well fall on our faces. We were, however, determined to take hold of the Web discussion practice in chat rooms, which was a common student recreational and personal communication activity and from this to see if there was any educational value in this medium and what effect it would have on language learning and communication skills. To do this, we had to get away from the 'anything goes' 'free for all' syndrome that has become the norm in Web chat rooms. Thus there had to be active teacher moderation and intervention as well as accountability.

We found that it was best for the groups to be password protected to raise the status of the discussion and to give some control over who could access the site and also give us the ability to monitor the appropriateness of what was being said. Along with this, we thought it was important to keep the groups small so that participants could pick up the tone and voice of the various contributors so it would in some way mirror face-to-face discussion.

It also seemed important that the discussions be run over a very limited time frame. The minds of some teenagers don't stay focused on the same topic for long so it is important to catch their enthusiasm and build on it. In the same way, many of us have found that a precious teachable moment in a classroom cannot be easily recreated some days later. We therefore wanted to generate some momentum but also limit the time commitment for teachers. It was not possible to expect busy professionals to prepare, teach and correct written work at the same time as monitoring the Web discussions of several groups of students on a daily basis. At the very least, we had to agree that the written contributions of students on screen were the only writing we would expect the students to do during that period and the only correcting that the teachers would do.

As a consequence of this decision by the teachers, the students undertaking the unit *In the Lake of the Woods* in Year 11 needed to know that their contributions to the discussion were accountable and would contribute to the assessment for the whole unit of work. We established very simple criteria for the teachers. One outcome from the Victorian Certificate of Education syllabus requires that:

> [The student should be able to] explore ideas and issues orally, giving considered reasons for a point of view and listening actively to the views of others.

*[In order to achieve this outcome,
the key skills the students will]
demonstrate include the ability to:*

- *follow and contribute to a
  discussion in a familiar setting;*
- *present evidence orally in support of
  a point of view;*
- *recognise and respond to cues for
  turn-taking in a discussion;*
- *listen actively and respond to others'
  views during a discussion;*
- *set own objectives for active
  participation in class discussion;*
- *record key points and questions
  raised during discussion'.*[11]

This did not preclude regular face-
to-face oral discussions, but we took a
broad view of the word 'orally', turning
this requirement into three simple
criteria:

- Did the student contribute to the
  discussion at least every second day?
- Did the student show evidence of a
  thorough knowledge of the text?
- Did the student respond constructively
  to the comments of others?

A chat-room model for biology or economics

A similar structure could easily be
applied to a discussion of one of the
many controversial topics in biology
or economics, and especially in similar
subjects which involve the teasing out
of ethical issues. 'Should native forests
be logged?', 'Will the deepening of
the shipping channel affect marine
life?', 'Should Australian kangaroos
be culled?', 'What are the risks and

advantages of genetic engineering?',
and many similar topics are commonly
discussed in senior secondary Biology
classes. Online discussion provides a
valid and alternative medium for these.

There will be issues that need to
be discussed from a range of points
of view in this type of discussion, as
opposed to problems that can be solved
simply. There are vested interests to
be accounted for, money restrictions,
pressure group influences and suchlike,
so students will learn that many things
are not scientifically neat and clinical
or easily determined. Take an issue
such as conflict over land use between
development, passive recreation and the
preservation of something historically
significant. Perhaps the class could
explore the land use upstream and the
consequences downstream. Students
often want to see a straightforward
solution, but unfortunately life is rarely
like that.

A chat-room model for art and art history

Similar controversial issues arise
frequently in Art and Art History
courses. This could range from a review
of a range of critics relating to the works
of a particular artist, the selection by a
curator of some works and not others,
or the hullabaloo over the staging of
certain exhibitions. The pulling of the
'Piss Christ' exhibit by Andreas Serrano
from an exhibition at the National
Gallery of Victoria in 1997 is a case
in point. More recently, a display of

art about the Israel–Palestine conflict was removed by the Melbourne City Council after complaints and threats of vandalism. Strongly worded letters to the newspapers included, '… we don't need the conflicts in the Middle East brought to Melbourne', 'What is the point of provoking discussion unless we are free to see and hear all points of view?' and '… are these the continuing symbols of oppression?'. The question of whether to use public money to support artists with a manifestly political agenda is a delicate one indeed. What a great opportunity to carry on that dialogue in class, either face-to-face or via a Web discussion, thus leaving more precious class time free for practical work.

Discussion groups using a front-end intranet organiser

Schools which have a front-end intranet organiser or similar software for organising curriculum material on the intranet will find that a discussion facility is incorporated in the program. If not, there are commercial programs such as ProBoards (http://www.proboards.com/index.html), mentioned in endnote 10, and most technical support staff will be glad to help teachers set up a discussion group. If these are not available, many schools use Microsoft Outlook for their e-mail. The public folders in this program can easily be set up as password-protected discussion sites for students within the same school.

Discussion group with colleagues

Why not set up a discussion just for a group of staff to test out the medium and experience what it is like to go to a discussion board each day and respond to the comments of others?

Here is a pertinent example from the tertiary area. Problem-based learning tutorials for medical students in a regional teaching centre are conducted in a room with just a projector, screen and one computer with wireless Web connection. Each week one student acts as the scribe and types up the discussion as it progresses. These notes are simultaneously displayed on the screen to the group. At the end of the tutorial, the summary and objectives for the week ahead are e-mailed to each member and the tutor. Between sessions, each member prepares a presentation, usually in Word, with added diagrams downloaded from teaching web sites and readily accessible online text books. At the start of the second session, each student's presentation is downloaded from their e-mail account and collated with all the others. Relevant discussion points are added during the teaching session by a scribe, then the overall document covering the original topic and all its learning objectives and the contributions of the group are again emailed to everyone before they leave the tutorial. No whiteboards, no paper, no overhead projectors! Copying from the work of other groups could become a

problem but this was not apparent in the
early days of this new way of learning.[12]
It is certainly a great stimulus for
discussion and interactive learning.

Endnotes

[1] P. Crawley, Principal, Knox Grammar School, Sydney. Address at the Expanding Learning Horizons
Conference, Lorne, Victoria, August 2002.

[2] L. Splitter & A. Sharp, *Teaching for better thinking*, ACER, Melbourne, 1995, p. 3.

[3] ibid., p. 182.

[4] 'Higher-order thinking', viewed 27 May 2004, <http://education.qld.gov.au/corporate/newbasics/
html/pedagogies/intellect/int1a.html>

[5] B. Schneiderman, *Leonardo's laptop: human needs and the new computing technologies*, MIT Press,
Cambridge Massachusetts, 2003, p. 121.

[6] J.G. Brooks, & M.G. Brooks, *In search of understanding: the case for constructivist classrooms*,
Alexandria, Virginia, ASCD, 1993, pp. 101–18.

[7] J. O'Donoghue, 'To cope, to contribute, to control' in A. Goodwyn (ed.), *English in the digital age:
information and communications technology and the teaching of English*, Cassell, 2000, p. 85.

[8] S. Godinho & B. Shrimpton, 'Boys' and girls' use of linguistic space in small group discussions: whose
talk dominates?' *Australian Journal of Language and Literacy*, Vol. 26, No. 3, 2003.

[9] K. Love, 'Mapping on-line discussion in senior English', *Journal of Adolescent and Adult Literacy*,
Vol. 45, No. 5, pp. 382–96.

[10] We used ProBoards for this discussion. See <http://www.proboards.com/index.html> See Appendix 2,
p. 158 for more details.

[11] See English Unit 1 Outcome 3, viewed 27 May 2004, <http://www.vcaa.vic.edu.au/vce/studies/english/
EnglishESLSD.pdf>

[12] Monash University Faculty of Medicine – Department of Rural Health at Traralgon Hospital.

Chapter 7

'Sustained lasting change in classroom performance is most likely to occur when teachers participate in a support network with partners ... in order to blend new teaching strategies into daily practice.'[1]

Hypertext:

A writing tool for lateral thinking

The learning and thinking context

What is hypertext and what can it mean to our day-to-day teaching? It is a new world of literacy where a document contains connections within itself to other documents. These can be to other pieces of text, as well as to sounds, images and movies. Images themselves can be selected to link to other sounds or documents. Viewers can zoom in on images or listen to audio annotations while viewing. The most significant feature of hypertext for a teacher and student is the control the viewer has over what is selected, viewed or heard, and in what order. Also, the content can be easily manipulated so that in some way the viewer becomes the author too. It is, in fact, a new way of interacting with text.

In her 1996 investigation, *Hypertext: the electronic labyrinth*, Ilana Snyder reminds us that the computer calls into question the traditional belief that the written text must take the form of a linear progression. 'The new electronic writing space,' she writes, 'allows a writer to entertain and present several lines of thought at once.'[2] Hypertext creates an open-bordered text, a text that cannot shut out other texts. It introduces randomness by decreasing control over its edges and borders, making it more self-contained and less dependent on what precedes and follows it. The printed book encourages us to think of the text as an organic whole, a unit of meaning independent of other texts, whereas hypertext gives us a unique opportunity to visualise intertextuality. It gives the opportunity to redefine beginnings and endings, and puts the focus back on the reader.[3]

In the realm of reading, literary hypertext can prompt questions about the nature of text and of reading, so its value as a learning tool in the English classroom is clear, despite the frustrations it brings to teachers.[4] Students probably take this multi-dimensional, mosaic reading environment for granted and wonder what all the fuss is about. They are attuned to boring down into web sites and picking up a variety of signals, even from a single computer screen. This is all quite apart from the text messages and mobile phonecalls they receive and send, and the music they listen to at the same time.

This chapter is more concerned about the production of text in a classroom as, for most students, the computer is a new writing surface that needs different conventions to those of the printed page. It is probable that hypertext writing will increasingly replace traditional linear text as the standard means of writing on a computer. It will allow the reader to determine where the beginning, middle and end of a piece lies and to plot their own way through the textual landscape. The reality is that we are speaking a new language, not just new words but a new way of using words.[5]

Students are able to interact electronically with texts so that they are not only reading but interpreting and making, with much greater control over the production process. Susan Boyce, a librarian, has located a publishing suite in her library to 'facilitate multimedia literacy, in much the same way that the photocopier, scanner and word processing facilities in the library had facilitated literacy in logo-centric, print modes of text'.[6] She sees the school library as a public space not tied to any faculty, readily accessible and with a rich bank of image and text support resources with permanent help on hand. The librarians in any school are, or should be, at the vanguard of the new literacies.

In similar vein, Tara Brabazon looks beyond the ungainly graft of electronic resources onto the 19th century models of print, space, time and information. She ridicules the libraries that reinvent themselves as information resource centres. This new name, she says, apparently means diverting money from the acquisition of books to maintaining database subscriptions. Her own vision is of librarians using their expertise to 'support new modes of reading, writing and communication, integrating and connecting discovery, searches, navigation and use of diverse resources'.[7]

Classroom strategies

Student familiarity with hypertext

Many of us may not have realised that students are intuitive users of hypertext, yet we often do not draw on this expertise to enrich and develop their learning. In 2001, we asked about 150 students over three year levels in a secondary school about their use of hypertext. The following table shows a summary by percentage of the total number of students and how they said they used hypertext.

Over 70 per cent said that they found hypertext useful to navigate, find things quickly, find their way around a long document, explore a topic, go quickly to a web site, and combine text and images. The disadvantages, a few said, were that the links did not always work and that some of their teachers did not know how to construct hyperlinks themselves.

I use hypertext:	Year 9		Year 10		Year 11	
	S	O	S	O	S	O
To find information on the Web	51	38	58	16	47	26
To click from one place to another on the Web	43	43	26	50	47	42
To explore Web pages	43	46	26	53	42	37
To have a word or piece of information explained in the Web	27	16	29	16	58	11
To have a word or piece of information explained in a CD-ROM	32	16	46	5	32	0
To make my own Web pages	19	11	11	11	16	11
To play computer games	22	8	16	5	21	0
To 'write' in Word and then I put in my own links	62	14	37	13	47	16
To put links into a PowerPoint presentation	19	5	26	5	26	16
As part of computer class activity	16	5	16	2	0	0
Note: (S = Sometimes, O = Often).						

Instructional writing using hypertext

In the rubric for a writing task in Year 11, we experimented by asking students to write an instructional piece with a specific audience focus.

Your piece must include at least five hyperlinks which could include images and text but there must be no more than one direct link to a web site.

*Here are some **suggestions** but you may choose **any topic** on which you have knowledge or expertise.*

- *Travel directions to a place you know well for a friend who wishes to go there.*
- *A recipe in a context, e.g. camp cooking for a Year 10 Outdoor Education Camp, or preparing for a birthday party of a close friend.*
- *How to get the most out of a visit to an art gallery. Write it for an insensitive Science student who is forced to go on a school excursion.*
- *Making a decision to purchase a second-hand car. Write this for your best friend who has just turned 18 and is itching to buy a car.*
- *A tourist brochure for a place you know well, for a backpacker from overseas.*
- *How to play a sport. Focus on a very specific aspect and skill (e.g. how experienced goalies take a penalty shoot-out in soccer). Write it for a Year 11 student who is keen to improve his or her skills.*
- *Any other topic and audience you may choose.*

A sporting hyperlink

One keen senior sportsman was eager to share his knowledge:

PLAYING A CRICKET COVER DRIVE!

Ever wondered why when you to try to hit a cover drive while playing cricket, it never comes off the right way?

Now you may be able to play a cover drive perfectly so you will not need to read this, but if your cover drive is not the best then just read on and I will tell you about the correct procedure of how to play a cover drive and some hints and tips on how to correct your shot. I guarantee you it will help you develop your shot better … it is your choice …Yes or No …

I am happy to see that you have decided to continue on reading my document. Firstly if you don't know what a cover drive is then click here to find out because if you don't then you won't understand most of what I am about to tell you.

For readers who wanted to know more and who clicked on the link above, the following information appeared on screen:

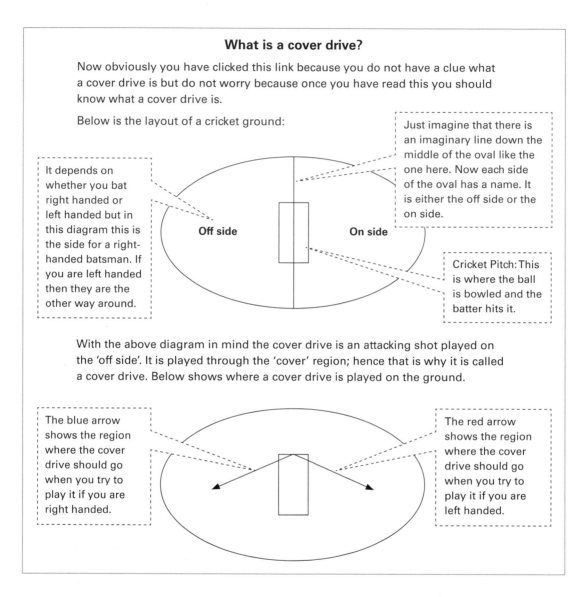

What is a cover drive?

Now obviously you have clicked this link because you do not have a clue what a cover drive is but do not worry because once you have read this you should know what a cover drive is.

Below is the layout of a cricket ground:

It depends on whether you bat right handed or left handed but in this diagram this is the side for a right-handed batsman. If you are left handed then they are the other way around.

Just imagine that there is an imaginary line down the middle of the oval like the one here. Now each side of the oval has a name. It is either the off side or the on side.

Off side

On side

Cricket Pitch: This is where the ball is bowled and the batter hits it.

With the above diagram in mind the cover drive is an attacking shot played on the 'off side'. It is played through the 'cover' region; hence that is why it is called a cover drive. Below shows where a cover drive is played on the ground.

The blue arrow shows the region where the cover drive should go when you try to play it if you are right handed.

The red arrow shows the region where the cover drive should go when you try to play it if you are left handed.

I hope this really helps you understand where a cover drive should be played and if you want to learn how to play it then go back to 'Playing a cricket cover drive' and continue reading the document.

The essay then continued with a paragraph each on the V grip, the stance and backswing, each one containing a link to diagrams the student had drawn himself. We asked students to include at least one live web site. This student concluded his essay by telling his readers to go to the Australian Cricket Board web site if they wanted any further coaching tips.

Italian holiday hyperlink

Another girl, who had been on a school cultural exchange to Italy, wrote advice for the following year's group and included links to the host school's web site, a list of common phrases in Italian to help the traveller, advice on how to avoid putting on extra kilos without offending the host mother and tongue-in-cheek advice on how to repel the advances of amorous Italian boys!

So you're stuck with an Italian host family for two weeks? Here's how to …

MAKE THE MOST OF YOUR STAY IN ITALY

Congratulations! You've successfully managed to get your parents to cough up the dough for you to go on the Italian exchange for … ahem … 'educational' purposes. But before you set off on this eye-opening experience, there are a few essentials you need to know. Read on …

Firstly, you need to know what to say. Try to avoid embarrassing mistakes such as replacing 'pomeriggio' (afternoon) with 'pomodoro' (tomato). Stick to basic language but still try to talk as much as possible – it is very flattering to the Italians when you at least attempt to speak their tongue. But BE CAREFUL – Italians do not speak like the actors on class tapes. They mumble just like the rest of us, and worst of all, many of them

speak a dialect … so when you thought you had a grasp of Italian, you basically have no idea. In saying that, still try your best for both your sake and theirs. There is nothing more uncomfortable than sitting at the dinner table in silence, so at least attempt to recount your daily activities ('Italia è bellissima!' usually wins them over; any patriot loves praise of his country). Here are some essential (and not so essential!) expressions to learn … ***CLICK***

The link included the following translated phrases, along with many more:

Italia è una paese bellissima! – Italy is a very beautiful country!
Può parlare più lentamente per favore? – Could you speak more slowly please?
Quanto costa? – How much is it?
Hai adocchiato quello? – Did you check out that guy?

You'll be given lots of time in the computer lab to send emails, so before you go take a speed-typing course there is never enough time to write to everyone. And most of all, while you're at school DON'T BE SNOBBISH! There is nothing worse than foreigners who seem stuck up, so when people yell out, 'ay, Canguri da Australia!' just laugh it off, it isn't meant maliciously. ***CLICK*** here to see the web site of the school you'll be attending, with pictures and everything!

… Hopefully this has been a useful guide to you … Before I go, you need to ***CLICK HERE*** for some invaluable info on general overseas etiquette. Have the best time in the world, and DON'T GET HOMESICK! Once you arrive home, everything is just the same as it's always been, so keep telling yourself that. Buona Fortuna…

This last link contained helpful advice, including:

> Remember to take only half the clothes you think you need and twice the money.
> Know at all times where your passport is, for a person without a passport is like a person without a country.

Informative writing

One student, who was fascinated by frogs, wrote his piece on bringing frogs back into the urban neighbourhood. He included paragraphs on providing a water source, indigenous plants and keeping domestic pets away, each hyperlinked to diagrams that he had drawn. He then included a table with sound files so that his readers could listen to the calls of the various species:

A key to identification – the frogs of Melbourne and surrounding suburbs

Common name	Scientific name	Call – click here to listen to the frogs
Common Froglet	*Crinia signifera*	'crick crick crick …'
Plains Froglet	*Crinia parinsignifera*	'eeeeeeeeek'
Red-groined Froglet	*Paracrinia haswelli*	'quack'
Victorian Smooth Froglet	*Geocrinia victoriana*	'wa-a-a-a-ark pip pip pip pip pip pip pip …'
Southern Toadlet	*Pseudophryne semimarmorata*	'cre-ek'
Bibron's Toadlet	*Pseudophryne bibroni*	'cre-ark'
Brown Tree Frog	*Litoria ewingi*	'creeee cree cree …'
Peron's Tree Frog	*Litoria peroni*	'cra-ah-ah-ah-ah …'
Growling Grass Frog	*Litoria raniformis*	'crawark-crawark-crok-crok'
Whistling Tree Frog	*Litoria verreauxi*	'weee weee weee …'
Eastern Banjo Frog	*Limnodynastes dumerili*	'bonk bonk po-ble-bonk po-ble-bonk …'
Spotted Marsh Frog	*Limnodynastes tasmaniensis*	'toc toc toc toc toc …'
Striped Marsh Frog	*Limnodynastes peroni*	'cluck cluck cluck …'
Common Spadefoot Toad	*Neobatrachus sudelli*	'craa-aw-aw-aw-aw-aw-aw-awk'

In other pieces, one student put in links to the daily weather reports on the ski fields, including the addresses and price lists of the ski-hire shops and a map of the best runs for the various levels of skiers. Another, who wrote a guide-book to a popular seaside holiday resort, included a list of restaurants, personal recommendations and links to a local entertainment guide. Another, who wrote a piece giving advice on how to pack for an outdoor education expedition, included links to photographs of himself in various stages of agony trying to stuff all his gear into his pack.

Hyperlinks in a Shakespeare text response

After the study of a Shakespeare text, one student, without prompting, presented an essay on 'Shylock, villain or victim', and decided to link what he wrote to the film *Life is Beautiful*. At the conclusion of his essay, he put in the following helpful links for the reader:

> If you would like more information on Shylock being a villain or a victim go to http://www.severi.org/studenti/ipertesti/jewish/merchant_of_venice.htm
>
> If you would like to know more about the movie *Life is Beautiful* go to http://www.amazon.com or http://www.geocities.com/aaronbcaldwell/Life.html

Another student wrote his final assessment piece on *The Merchant of Venice*, but included, at his own volition, links to previous class work he had done and to current productions of the play in the United Kingdom and the United States. These turned the piece into quite a different kind of essay, though the essential arguments on the topic were included and very clear.

Writing in this way and teasing out ideas will be a strength, certainly not a disadvantage, when it comes to writing a traditional essay in the final Year 12 examination. Interestingly, the Victorian Curriculum and Assessment Authority was preparing for 1300 students to trial the computers for their final external English examination in 2004 so that they could compare the performance of those using computers with those using pen and paper, and what effect this would have on the way the markers responded.[8] The report added that one of the driving factors of this test run was the concern expressed by some schools that their computer-literate students could be disadvantaged by pen and paper exams. A later report suggested that examinations could be online for all 80,000 students within five years. A Chemistry trial in June 2004, where papers were marked both online and off-line, found no difference in marks. In a trial later the same year, 2000 English and Mathematics students from 20 schools sat one examination online and another using pen and paper under normal examination conditions. Both papers were double marked as they would be at a final examination but results were not available at the time of writing.[9]

How do we assess this kind of writing?

In the instructional task outlined above, the students were given the criteria on which their work would be assessed in advance. This involved a lot of faculty discussion as we needed to agree on whether we were assessing their technical competence with computers or their ability to write and deal with the topic. Were we asking for hyperlinks as a gimmick or as an essential element in this kind of writing? The conclusion was that the hyperlinks would be an attention-grabber for the teachers because the territory was so unfamiliar and would definitely be a technical challenge for us. For the students, however, it was a natural part of what they might expect to do and the requirement did not seem to faze them at all. The table opposite shows the criteria we finally agreed upon. Note the emphasis on the quality of the information and the language features and conventions in the writing. We tried to judge the main piece and the linked documents as a whole, and only in the area of coherence and organisation did we look at the appropriateness of the hyperlinks.

A more serious issue for teachers than agreeing on the criteria was the very practical issue of how to collect and correct this kind of work. The teacher who wants to gather only handwritten or printed work to take home and mark as they curl up by the fire, red wine in one hand and red pencil in the other, cannot do so with this kind of writing.

From a practical point of view, students who use hyperlinked writing must gather all the related documents into one folder. This can then be transferred as a complete folder to the teacher either by disc or memory stick, infra-red transfer or by lodging it on the school's network in a 'common drive', accessible by both teacher and student. E-mail is not suitable for this purpose as only single documents can be attached to an e-mail message. Therefore, issues of online correction and classroom and student management (Chapter 10) become significant factors if teachers are going to go down this track.

Criteria for assessment	VH*	H	M	L	VL/NS
Criterion 1 – Knowledge and control of the chosen content Quality and usefulness of the instructional information. Evidence of research and sound grasp of the subject matter.					
Criterion 2 – **Language features appropriate to purpose and audience** The reader could confidently follow the directions or instructions. Extent to which writing captures the interest and attention of the reader.					
Criterion 3 – **Conventions of the English language** Basics and mechanics of expression. Effective and accurate language appropriate to specific purpose and audience. Expressiveness and fluency.					
Criterion 4 – Coherence and effective organisation Usefulness and relevance of the information attached by the hyperlinks. Extent to which hyperlinks interrupt or add to the basic material. Was the hyperlinked material appropriate or should it have been in the main text? Did the hyperlinks work? Structure and organisation of the written material.					
Grade awarded					
* VH = very high, H = high, M = medium, L = low, VL/NS = very low/not shown					

Wider applications and suggested activities

There are some great new ways to increase the repertoire of student responses. We live in a world of changing literacy. Recognising that many students no longer think and write in the ways that we as teachers used to, we need to think beyond the straightjacket of the linear essay tradition and give students the freedom to 'think outside the square', making it clear to them that we welcome a range of responses and will, in fact, reward innovative thinking and writing.

Various ways of responding to poetry (or any other text in virtually any subject) were outlined in Chapter 4. To that list we could now add hyperlinks. Students could be asked to identify phrases or words and hyperlink them to pictures, explanations or glossaries or some other document that may indicate the student's personal response or demonstrate understanding of the work.

There is an example of a Year 9 History unit on World War II in Chapter 11. The students were required to hyperlink elements of their class study to the final assessment essay.

Experimenting with hyperlinks

Try a hyperlinking task for yourself as a trial run. To do this, create a new folder called *Hyperlink Trial*.

- Open any existing document on your My Documents and Save As in the *Hyperlink Trial* folder.
- Open any existing second document and Save As in the same folder.
- Select any words in the first document, then use Insert/Hyperlink OR Ctrl K to link it to the second document.
- Now open the second document, type at the bottom *Return to Document 1*, select the phrase and put in a link back to the *Document 1*.
- Do the same to one or two more documents that you copy into your folder and also put in the reverse hyperlink.
- Now put in a ***link to one of the web sites*** you know and have saved in your *Favourites* folder.

As mentioned earlier, when you do this with students they must keep all the linked documents in one folder and give the whole folder to you when they submit it for marking, otherwise the hyperlinks will not work.

History hyperlink example

Try asking students to create two stories about two schoolboys, one living today and one living in the time of Ancient Rome or Egypt or Greece. Hyperlinks could be used to enable readers to slide through time, jumping between the stories at various points.[10]

Geography fact sheet

In another possible activity, students could be asked to research a country by preparing a fact sheet. When they are ready, they prepare a board game where the clues are hidden with hyperlinks. This is a SchoolKiT activity with one page of the instructions as follows:

Hiding in Asia

Now that you have performed your research and have written your clue statements, it is time to hide yourself and see whether your partner can find you.

To open the Map, click this button:

The Map workbook contains two worksheets. The Board worksheet is where your partner is going to guess your location. The Hidden worksheet is where you are going to hide yourself.

At the bottom of the worksheet, click on the Hidden tab.

You will use a formula to represent your hidden location on the map. The formula looks like this:

=IF(Board!A4='g','Fred',")

The Formula Explained

Let's try one together as a way to explain the formula.

On the Hidden worksheet, click in cell A4 and enter the above formula.

This formula says: If, on the Board worksheet, your partner types in cell A4 the letter g ('g' stands for the word 'guess') then show the name Fred (this will be your name). Otherwise, show nothing.[11]

The examples in Chapter 11, where students submit an assignment with required hyperlinks, is applicable for almost any subject. In these tasks we required our students to prepare an assignment, including within the main document links to a glossary, a formula table, a live web site, a cartoon, a document summarising some previous learning and so on. However, beware when you ask students to submit an assignment like this. Such hyperlinked documents cannot be printed and they make no sense unless the teacher is prepared and able to mark them online. This topic is dealt with more fully in Chapter 10.

Endnotes

[1] J. McKenzie, *How teachers learn technology best*, FNO Press, 1999, p. 36.

[2] I. Snyder, *Hypertext: the electronic labyrinth*, Melbourne University Press, Melbourne, 1996, p. 45.

[3] ibid., pp. 50–7.

[4] G. Parr, 'If in a literary hypertext a traveller…' in Durrant & Beavis, *P(ICT)URES of ENGLISH – Teachers, learners and technology*, Australian Association for the Teaching of English, Adelaide, 2001, p. 229.

[5] G. Kelly, *Retrofuture: rediscovering our roots, recharting our routes*, InterVarsity Press, Illinois, 1999, pp. 88, 89.

[6] S. Boyce, 'Engineering literacy in the library' in C. Durrant & C. Beavis, 2001, op. cit., p. 136.

[7] T. Brabazon, *Digital hemlock: Internet education and the poisoning of teaching*, UNSW Press, 2002, p. 93.

[8] *The Sunday Age*, 6 June 2004, p. 7.

[9] *The Sunday Age*, 17 October 2004, p. 9.

[10] This suggestion is from a SchoolKiT module. For further details see http://www.edclass.com and the explanation in Chapter 9.

[11] From the SchoolKiT activity 'Where in Asia am I?' for Years 6–9 Geography. The rubric of the activity says: 'Asia is the planet's largest continent. In this activity you will hide yourself in a country in Asia. Your partner must try and find you by using clue statements that you provide. Will your partner be successful?' For further details see http://www.edclass.com and further explanation on page 158.

Chapter 8

'[Leonardo da Vinci's] notebook pages demonstrate the benefits of integrating graphics and text, and his analyses testify to the power of combining visual and analytic thinking. [550 years later,] this combination of skills inspires us – this time to envision information and communication technologies that are in harmony with human needs.'[1]

Visual literacies: Moving on from predominantly text-based learning

The learning and thinking context

'Screenagers' of today absorb information from a far wider range of media than their teachers can even begin to imagine, and they transmit their own messages through visual, auditory and printed means in ways that leave older generations gasping to keep up. There is an increasing use of visual text in society, so there is a significant need for teachers to address these areas in the classroom.

The speed of change has left many of us almost breathless. For example, the study of film as text rather than studying the film of the book is now the norm for many English classes, and students are becoming as adept at creating and manipulating images onscreen as they are at dealing with text. Bill Green now calls it a 'digital convergence of technology, literacy and the arts ... as we develop new attitudes towards textual practices that are appropriate for a mixed media, multi-semiotic, digital-electronic environment'.[2]

The corollary of these developments is that if students can control images on their screens, so can the mass media in a very powerful way. It is, therefore, all the more important that we teach discrimination skills and critical thinking. Media texts can so easily be 'manipulated, copied, excerpted, morphed, revised, annotated ... and may contain messages that ... harbour bias, specific ideologies or prejudices of all kinds – racial, economic, gender, political and moral.'[3] Semali makes a strong point that popular culture can glamorise violence, irresponsible sex, junk food consumption, drugs and alcohol, while stereotyping the boring teacher, the geeky egghead male adolescent, the airhead blonde, the welfare mother, clueless father, and so on. He reminds us how easy it is to 'manipulate media texts and worldview to privilege one viewpoint over another ... thus teachers need to understand more about what students already know before they start to teach what they think students ought to know'.[4]

Of course, such manipulation has always occurred, but it appears to be so much more blatant and intrusive in a multimedia environment. There is also the added concern that a lot of information is passively pushed at students who do not need to interact with it but just absorb it, and it comes at such a rate that they may have no time to filter and align it with their own developing world view.

Perhaps all history students should view the web site 'The Commissar Vanishes', which shows a series of images of Stalin deliberately manipulated as his regime continued from 1939 to 1953. The web site says of itself,

> *The Commissar Vanishes exhibition explores this censored history. By the 1930s Communist 'truth' circulates worldwide in party approved books. With airbrush or ink spot, the photo censors work quietly. But despite their power, they ultimately fail. The images expose decades of photographic lies.*[5]

Schneiderman puts forward a similar perspective when he says that listening to radio and CDs, and watching TV and videotapes are not educational panaceas as they are

> *largely passive media, offering limited capability for students to be creative unless educators shift their focus to student content generation using these media. Once again it is taking decades for educators to recognise that the most potent use of videotapes happens when teachers offer blank ones to students.*[6]

Classroom strategies

Accessing the immediate

Current text books for the study of media language and the presentation of issues drag out the still important but well-worn topics of whales, gun licences and capital punishment. With online access, the issues can surely be much more immediate and capture the interest of the students in a way that even the best prepared printed text can never do.

On the day of the Columbine massacre in April 1999, when 13 secondary students were gunned down by two of their peers, I happened to be teaching a Year 8 class in a computer lab. The students brainstormed the titles of national and overseas newspapers and then worked in pairs, one searching any national newspaper while their partner searched one from overseas for news of the massacre. The pair then swapped seats to compare the stories, and were surprised to find that most of the reports were identical, varying only in the degree of detail. Only one report that any student found made a reference to the home and family of the accused gunmen.

It can be especially difficult to find a topic where the information is accessible and able to capture the interest of a group of lower secondary students. The confluence of text, pictures, maps and interviews on this occasion made a compelling jumping-off point for some valuable lessons about the media, as well as giving students an understanding of how news is reported in different parts of the world. Web sites of most world newspapers are given on page 48.

Mark Latham became the leader of the Australian Labor Party on 2 December 2003 by a single vote in the party room, and to many people's surprise, suddenly became the potential prime minister with an election less than a year away. The cartoonists had a field day. What a great and immediate opportunity for students to compare his portrayal by various cartoonists and to make a close analysis of the visual language.

This is how Moir in the *Sydney Morning Herald* portrayed the issue:

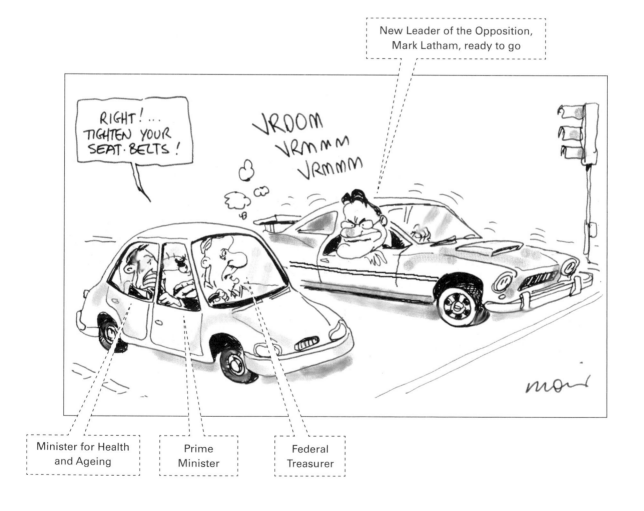

In Melbourne's *The Age* newspaper, Spooner used similar car race imagery on the same day but added the frequently quoted Latham metaphor about the ladder of opportunity.

Leader of the Opposition, Mark Latham, 2003

Deputy Leader of the Opposition (2003) with Mark Latham's 'ladder of opportunity' in a tradesman's vehicle

Federal Treasurer 2003

Prime Minister 2003

Nicholson in *The Australian* took quite a different line, with Latham escaping from the chrysalis while the current Prime Minister and his Cabinet colleagues rush around trying to catch the pesky insect with venerated Labor figures from the past looking up at Latham in admiration.

The challenge of cartoon analysis

Some recent research has concluded that 'learning and information environments must provide the scaffolding that supports critical and creative thinking, especially in the light of opportunities and threats that learning technologies can bring'.[7]

Prime Minister and Federal Treasurer

Minister for Health and Ageing, and Minister for Foreign Affairs

Mark Latham, new Leader of the Opposition

Former Prime Minister and mentor for Mark Latham with leading Opposition figures

Cartoon by Nicholson from *The Australian*. <http://www.nicholsoncartoons.com.au>

In 2002, a Year 9 class was set the following task:

> *Find a **current cartoon** from an American newspaper which is on a theme of relevance to Australia. **Copy and paste it here**, then in a paragraph below or using callout boxes to annotate, **sum up the contention or message of the cartoonist**. What is he or she communicating? In what way is the reader being positioned to believe or agree with something? This web site may help you http://cagle.slate.msn.com/*

The topic in the news at the time, and selected by one student, was the Washington sniper. Here is how that student responded:

From a teacher's point of view, we were impressed that this student was able to make a selection on a topic that interested him, could pick up the subtleties of the message and respond to the details of the cartoon. This can be a difficult task as all of us are quick to laugh at cartoons but often find it tricky to put into words their contention and say how the fine points of the drawing contribute to our understanding.

Bullets emphasise the danger of inner city crime.

Inner cities sign – Nothing published or done about the daily shootings of innocents in inner cities.

Key point: suburbans safe but inner city citizens in as much danger as ever.

Sarcasm – sniper problem eliminated but street crime still unsafe

The study of a still from a movie

Studying a film text can be frustrating as we repeatedly trawl through the movie to show the class key scenes and focus on the detail of any one aspect, just as we would do by getting students to look at a particular paragraph in a novel. DVDs are gradually alleviating this problem but it may still be some time before we either have easy access to DVD players in our schools or the films we want to teach are available.

In a recent study of *The Shawshank Redemption*, students were asked to select a still frame from a number of images that had been made available on the school's intranet. They were then asked to make a series of assertions about the shot they chose. This was the 'who, where, what, why and when' scenario, as well as what the shot was telling us about characters and plot at that point in the film. One student made some interesting assertions about the crucial scene where the warden discovers the escape tunnel used by the prisoner:

The camera view is from Andy's perspective looking up on the look of horror on Norton's and Hadley's faces

Image is when warden realises that Andy has escaped and all hell is about to break loose for him.

This shot shows the beginning of the fall of power in the movie. Norton is the main person in shot with Hadley in the background. They are the only people in the shot because they controlled every aspect of authority within the prison – Andy's escape will affect them the most.

The shot pans away – down the tunnel. This symbolises Andy crawling away, and also shows the Warden's control on the prison is slipping away.

This kind of response does not preclude formal written assessment, but as a homework exercise or classroom response tool, it confirmed basic understandings and it was certainly enjoyable for the students to be able to express themselves in this very succinct way.

Other text study incorporating visual responses

As part of a study on the language of advertising, students could use PowerPoint or another graphic program to devise an advertisement for a fictitious product which they would like to create and market. For assessment, they simply show these to the class on-screen, with an opportunity to also explain the design principles they have incorporated – why certain colours have been chosen, size of font, language that appealed to a particular target market, and so on.

This is an example of what one student created:

In place of a written book report on a wide-reading fiction book from the library, students enjoy producing a poster that advertises a meeting of the fan club for this author. Here is a suggested rubric for the task:

You are the president of a fan club for your favourite author. You have read at least two of this author's books including one during the last weeks.

Eager for literary discussion and the promotion of the author's works, you decide to create some promotional materials to target and encourage others to read some of the novels and join your fan club.

To attract members, you do three things:

- *Design a new advertisement for the fan club*
- *Create a FAQ (Frequently Asked Questions List) to distribute to new members*
- *Write two monthly newsletters highlighting a different novel each month to stimulate discussion.*

Reflect on the effectiveness of your work as President.

One student accessed the publisher's web site for a contact address and used it to e-mail the writer directly with a series of questions. She was delighted to get a brief and apparently personal response within a few days. This student was not only commended for her initiative but had some valuable information to add to her poster. Here is the beginning of a poster about one student's favourite author:

Why other people should read this book

This book is just pure enjoyment to read so all of us recommend it

One student, when asked to present the main ideas of a chapter of a class novel, used a simple Paint program in Windows to create the following image to represent an Aboriginal initiate being taught to fish by his tribal uncle but being caught by a shark instead of catching a dugong. This is from the first chapter of Alan Baillie's novel *Songman*:

Another student, who was reading a book that made reference to the spirit world, decided to send an e-mail to a US society for mediums to satisfy his curiosity. They wisely asked his age and only gave him a brief response while the teacher, who found out what he was doing, suggested to his parents that they monitor his interests. Another student used the Web address in the novel to contact the writer directly and was thrilled to get a detailed reply in less than 24 hours.

Linking the visual to the verbal

When teachers try to stimulate ideas for creative writing, the real challenge may be just confronting the blank page. Try giving students a digital camera for recess or lunch or a sporting match. A student who can come back to class with a picture of an altercation in the canteen queue or the staged picture of a body outside the Principal's office window can paste it into a Word document. What a great starting point for a piece of writing. Pictures from the Web offer similar unlimited options. A series of pictures could be used as prompts for a narrative or students could be asked to illustrate their story with pictures that are incorporated into the text of a hyperlinked piece of writing.

This is the rubric for one task we tried:

You are a novelist deciding on a plot for a new novel.

Choose from the Internet or Clip Art, or any other source you wish, the following:

- *two characters or people*
- *two objects or images or things of some kind*
- *one place or background setting.*

Lay these images out *on a single A4 page.*

*Now write a **300–400 word plot summary** or **synopsis** for your planned story. Remember that you will be using this summary to sell your idea to a publisher who will be asked to fund your work while you write the novel over a period of 12 months.*

Your synopsis will include at least the following elements:

- *The names and brief details about each character*
- *The relationship between the characters before and during the action of the story*
- *Enough details of the setting to give the reader a clear background for the action*
- *The action or plot of the story.*

These are the elements that one student chose from readily available Clip Art without going to picture web sites:

He then wrote a synopsis to accompany these graphics:

> It is set in the mountains on the Himalayas in winter, high winds are ruminating everywhere and it is set back in the time of peasants and so forth …
>
> The main storyline of the book is when a very old poor man, who has no home, no money and no belongings, resorts to stealing, otherwise he will die of starvation. While he is trying to steal the money (which is successful) he gets caught, but using his defensive skills he breaks through their armies into the wilderness of the snowy weather where there are lots of men on horses out, ready to kill the robber at first sight. He gets away successfully at first when he finds a hut in which he finds a unique knife, which he uses to defend himself when the robbers find him again after a desperate search for their money and the robber who would get killed. The robber gets away again successfully and manages to live life on the rich side. He changes his name so the men on the horses do not know where to find him and capture him.

Visual responses to poetry

It is helpful to give tight directions to students who need them, but we have also tried to make the tasks as open-ended as possible so that capable students have some latitude to follow up their own interests.

In a war poetry unit around the time of Anzac Day, we gave the students about 20 poems, read through them in class, discussed them and 'taught' them in the traditional way. However, we then gave the following open-ended response task for class work and homework:

Annotate any one poem in a document called 'Poetry Response'.

You will do this in a single A4 sheet by using at least:
- *6 Callout boxes OR footnotes OR text boxes OR images.*
- *and at least one picture which illustrates the mood or idea or setting of the poem.*

Find your own images but you may wish to look at
- *The Fine Arts Museum of San Francisco at http://www.famsf.org/*
or
- *our national picture web site at http://www.pictureaustralia.org/ with pictures from our National Library, Australian War Memorial, the National Archives, Fryer Library of Uni of Qld and the State Libraries of Vic, Tas and NSW.*

Try Google pictures or Alta Vista images or http://www.ditto.com/ OR web site image search or image search in other search engines.

In these annotations, you will be writing altogether between 200 and 250 words of comment about the poem.

Your annotations may include some or all or none of the following:
- *Imagery through simile and metaphor and personification.*
- *Imagery through the use of particular adverbs and adjectives.*
- *Other imagery.*
- *Communication through rhythm and sound.*
- *Appeals to the senses.*

- *Connections and reversals.*
- *The use of direct speech and monologue.*
- *Patterns or repetitions or the use of symbols.*

Remember, your teachers are NOT INTERESTED in how clever you are at identifying poetic devices. We ARE INTERESTED in your personal response to the poems you have chosen and how clearly you can communicate that response to the reader.

One Year 9 student, whose work had been modest up to this point, decided to show his understanding of the poem 'But you didn't' by Merrill Glass by drawing a series of cartoons, shown below, in the Microsoft Paint program to illustrate each verse.

Just in case the reader didn't understand his drawings, he continued with the following explanation:

This poem is really interesting. That is why I particularly chose it. The start of the first three paragraphs in the poem commences with 'Remember the time' and it concludes with 'But you didn't'. What makes the poem 'But You Didn't' great is the way it builds up to a short, disturbing and sad conclusion. It portrays a girl who took most things for granted, but didn't notice how much her boyfriend put up with her until he died an honourable death.

A Year 11 student with limited skills in written communication but a great interest in visual literacy and competence with the Corel Draw program from his Art classes, decided to illustrate the same poem but in a different way:

> Remember the time I forgot to tell you the dance was
>
> Formal, and you wore jeans?
>
> I thought you'd hate me ...
>
> But you didn't.

For the next verse:

> Remember the times I'd flirt with
>
> Other boys just to make you jealous, and
>
> You were?
>
> I thought you'd drop me ...
>
> But you didn't.

He also prepared a collage of photos of himself with his best mate's girlfriend at a party just to make his response really personal. He then went on to annotate the poem with callouts to show what particular features of it meant to him. The result was not profound but it engaged him like no previous task had done so far in that class.

Wider applications and suggested activities

A novel path to political, geographical and cultural research

A Year 10 class was recently studying the biographical novel *Off the Rails* by Chris Hatherly and Tim Cope about a 12-month trip on a recumbent bicycle across the former Soviet Union. As part of the introduction to the novel and an opportunity for students to familiarise themselves with the political, geographical and cultural background to the trip, the students were given a brief research task with the following instructions:

You will present your report in any appropriate manner depending on the topic you choose. It could, for example, be a 400–500 word essay in Word OR a report in Publisher combining text and images OR a PowerPoint presentation with images, graphics and sound and at least 50 words of text in the speaker's notes explaining each slide OR an Inspiration diagram where you tease out one of the themes in the novel and have a total of at least 300 words in the Add Notes boxes.

We encouraged the students to select any topic that interested them, but if they could not find something we gave a list of suggestions. We try never to integrate technology for the sake of it, just ensure that students have the basic skills – and most do anyway when they come from primary school these days. They are then in a position to choose for themselves a way of responding that is most appropriate to the task. This is part of the rubric:

1 Import a map of Asia from an e-atlas and mark in the key places Tim and Chris visited on their journey. Annotate the map with details of significant events that occurred in at least six places, using text boxes and arrows or callouts. You will be writing a total of over 200 words in the boxes.

2 Research the restrictions on tourist travel within China and comment on the specific ways in which Tim and Chris flouted the restrictions.

3 Why couldn't this trip within Russia have happened 20 years earlier?

4 Review the life of the Russian President Vladimir Putin and the recent election. What are his policies and what do you predict about the future of Russia under his leadership?

5 Examine the art of Russia. Go to galleries online in Russia and the west and prepare a report on any one great Russian artist. This will include some visual material, some biographical material and some appraisal of the artist's work.

6 Do the same as No 5 but with one of the great Russian composers.

7 Write an argumentative essay on the topic, 'Democracy will not work in Russia'.

8 Choose any ONE place that was important to Chris and Tim on their journey, such as Babushkina, the Taiga forest, Siberia, Kirov, Taishet, the BAM railway, the Altai mountains, the Gobi desert or any other place that you thought was significant. Write a detailed account of what happened there with appropriate illustrations.

9 Make up a topic which interests you.

One student with a particular interest in art chose the topic of realism in 17th-century Russian art and was very keen for his peers to see the slides he had prepared. Readers may argue that this is an Art rather than an English exercise but it seemed to us that we were stimulating cross-curriculum thinking and enriching this boy's understanding of the text, while allowing him to draw on his art skills and interests.

Computers make multi-disciplinary tasks like this much easier to initiate and manage; the outcomes can be exciting for both the teacher and student.

There is plenty of material on the Web to act as stimulus to lateral ideas for written and visual responses. Unfortunately the Web can also be a huge time waster and a source of great frustration. Remember to always have a 'Favourites' column set up in your Internet Browser with subheadings like drawers in a filing cabinet labelled to take the material. It also needs the ready support of colleagues to willingly pass on any good sites they have found, hopefully with some helpful annotations so that you don't need to reinvent the wheel.

Three are worth mentioning:

A brilliant site for students in about Years 6 to 9 with ideas for starting a piece of writing, brainstorming a topic, keeping a writing journal, working through the drafting process etc: http://www.writesite.org/

Try the mystery writing site: http://www.mysterynet.com/learn/ as a starting point for a piece of writing.

It can also be great fun to get students to write 55-word stories, a task which will challenge the garrulous and focus their minds on the structure of a short story. There are plenty of examples around, including a daily story from a reader in the Melbourne *Herald Sun*. One is the best is *The New Times – the San Luis Obispo County's News and Entertainment Weekly*, who say they invented the genre and have been running a competition for 16 years: http://www.newtimes-slo.com/index.php?p=55fiction

But more of this in the next chapter!

Using online resources

One of the best-produced and most stimulating CD-ROM resources available to English teachers is *Five Bells*,[8] which is called an 'interactive celebration of Australia's favourite poem'. It includes some biographical material on Kenneth Slessor, several voices reading five of his best-known short poems with musical accompaniment and a ten-minute-long

movie where the poem *Five Bells* is read to the complement of film clips and voice. Asking students to bring earphones and access the CD from the network is a very enjoyable experience for them.

When we used this resource, we gave the students a response sheet to fill out so that there was some structure and purpose to their listening. This is particularly important with a boys' class. Topics included:

Some significant facts I learnt about the life of Slessor.

Some significant facts I learnt about the life and work and death of Joe Lynch.

Some significant facts about the poem Five Bells – e.g. when it was written, what prompted the writing, what it is about.

I read and heard at least two of Slessor's poems. Here are some notable images or phrases or repetitions or key words or other things I would like to comment on:

Poem 1:

Poem 2:

The examples in this chapter could be applied to many subjects, for example, illustrating a cartoon in a history class or annotating a photograph of a land formation in a Geography class, especially where the photograph has been taken on an actual field trip.

Designing a memorial

One interesting and challenging activity in SchoolKiT[9] is *Designing a Memorial*. The task asks students to:

imagine that you have been commissioned to design a memorial wall to commemorate a significant event in history. To complete this activity, you will undertake research to learn all that you can about the subject of the memorial, then use what you have learned to create a moving and informative tribute.

A PowerPoint example explains the principles of researching and designing a memorial with this instruction:

As you develop your memorial wall, keep in mind your goals. Depending on the context, your aim may be:

- *to encourage remembrance;*
- *to honour and express gratitude;*
- *to encourage reflection;*
- *to educate;*
- *to preserve history and cultural heritage; and/or*
- *to inspire national pride.*

Then there are instructions on how to format the page, build the stone wall as a background, put in a text box, engrave the text and make the sculpture stand out as a relief against the background.

Virtual museum of history

Another activity which History and Social Studies teachers would find very stimulating for students in about Years 6 to 9 is called *Virtual Museum of History*. In this, students are asked to

create an historical exhibit with information based on four general themes: History Timeline, Geography, Society/Culture, and Artefacts/Evidence.

To complete this activity you will:

- *select a person, event, or culture to study;*
- *research information based on the four theme areas;*
- *edit and write research so that it can be read by people from the ages of 10 to 60;*
- *create an electronic virtual museum exhibit.*

Students are then given a sample virtual exhibit on the Aztecs and instructions on deciding upon their own topic, preparing a data sheet, selecting information, building the exhibit, creating a floor and background, adding exhibits and using action buttons in PowerPoint.[10] By the end of this task students will know a lot more about their chosen topic, have acquired some new computer skills and presented their information in both visual and verbal form.

Aboriginal history or Australian Studies exercise

History educators who teach Aboriginal history or Australian Studies may like to track down a superb two CD-ROM set *Frontier – Stories from White Australia's Forgotten War*.[11] It includes 90 minutes of video and audio by leading Australian actors, excerpts from some 150 primary sources, 200 paintings, illustrations and photographs, internet sites, suggestions for further reading and a search index. A great resource like this can be an infectious motivator for both teacher and student.

Endnotes

1 B. Schneiderman, *Leonardo's laptop: human needs and the new computing technologies*, MIT Press, Cambridge, Massachusetts, 2003, p. 4.

2 C. Durrant & C. Beavis, *P(ICT)URES of ENGLISH – Teachers, learners and technology*, Australian Association for the Teaching of English, Adelaide, 2001 p. 8.

3 M. Semali, 'Crossing the information highway: the web of meanings and bias in global media', viewed 7 January 2003, <http://www.readingonline.org/newliteracies/semali3/index.html>

4 ibid.

5 Viewed 10 May 2004, <http://www.newseum.org/berlinwall/commissar_vanishes>

6 B. Schneiderman, 2003, op. cit., p. 118.

7 V. Watson & M. Kairouz, 'Student learning and information processing in the knowledge age: a case for the strategic teaching of thinking skills', IARTV Occasional Paper No. 75, May 2002, Melbourne.

8 K. Slessor, *Five Bells*, produced by Roar Films in conjunction with G3 and the support of the Australian Film Commission and Arts Australia.

9 For further details see http://www.edclass.com and the explanation on page 158.

10 ibid.

11 *Frontier – Stories from Australia's Forgotten War*, two CD-ROM set, Australian Broadcasting Commission.

Chapter 9

'The new knowledge economy demands that we learn by our direct confrontation with information that is increasingly accessed, or delivered, electronically. Therefore the need to teach explicitly the processes and skills of thinking has become critical.'[1]

Critical use of the World Wide Web

The learning and thinking context

What makes the Web so fascinating?
Why do otherwise balanced and normal
adults become mesmerised in front of
a computer screen? Is it the curiosity of
what is out there? Are we such a prurient
generation that we just can't keep away
from the multitude of porn sites? Is
finding a needle in a haystack on the Web
like doing a home handyman job that
won't work, so we keep trying again and
again in the hope of getting it right?

We recognise that students, who
have been brought up with the Web
as a normal part of their lives, see it
quite differently to adults, for whom it
is often a mystery and fascination. It is
important, however, that we do not just
see the Web as text on a screen and a
quicker access to information. It actually
provides a whole new way of integrating
text, image and sound, while giving users
a greater control over what they do and
how they do it.

Ease of publication on the Web is also
one of its practical uses for teachers.
English and Humanities teachers in
particular are always keen for students to
write to a real audience and are delighted
when they see a student's article in the
local newspaper or a reply to the class

from a sports coach when a student
has perhaps written to query an unfair
result or the rules for a carnival. How
much easier it is to write for an audience,
published internally on the school's
intranet or on the Web, provided there
are safeguards for anonymity.

The Web helps us to move away from
the traditional notions of the written
word to an understanding of the word as
part of a matrix of communication. Jane
O'Donoghue writes that

*appropriate use of ICT can help us
to put students at the forefront of
producing texts ... Writing for the
Web, a student is not obliged to
have an interior need to write, nor
even to have an audience to write
for. The fact that anyone can publish
anything means that the notion of
audience is denied, the concept of text
is decentralized and the process itself
becomes the focus.*[2]

Schneiderman takes this one step
further when he says 'the Web enables
students to publish their projects, making
them available for anyone. Students are
anxious about making their work so
visible, but it does push them to polish
their projects more than in the past'.[3]

Classroom strategies

Teaching good analysis skills

We can't take it for granted that students will know how to search the Web effectively any more than that they will know how to structure an essay, respond to a poem, find relevant material for research, use a dictionary, interpret the latest trade figures or follow the patterns in a novel without some guidance. If, for example, we ask students to analyse and annotate a web site, we need to tell them what to look for: use of colour, simplicity of layout, ease of exploration; direct them to the links and to the usefulness of the information on the splash page; ask for the date on which the page was last updated, the name of the author or Web master and especially ask them to verify the quality of the information.

We could summarise this into a series of questions such as:
- Who created the web site?
- What is it about?
- Where was it created?
- When it was last updated?
- How reliable is the information and how do we know?[4]

Of course, this process could be reversed by the teacher annotating a web site, then sending that model annotation to the students so that they can review the accuracy of what the teacher has done. Similarly, groups of students at the start of a project or unit of study could each be given a different web site to find, explore and report on. From this, an annotated list of useful resources can be collated and given to all students. A step like this could save a huge amount of wasted time, let alone the possibility of limiting frustration levels.

Coping with frustration

The Web can be an enormous time waster, so many students, not to mention their teachers, end up angry and frustrated after a session of Web searching (or was it just vague Net grazing that they were doing?). Some of the following suggestions may help:
- Library resources and class texts should be carefully vetted, selected and offered for reading and research at a level appropriate to the age and conceptual understanding of the user, so we know that when we go to them we will find relevant and usable information. By comparison, we must be aware that the internet has the potential to drown us in garbage. Jamie McKenzie writes,
Many teachers will find the Internet too poorly structured to support efficient learning unless we invest in lesson and unit development that meets their desire for order and practicality. Teachers seek structured lessons and scaffolding to deliver efficiency, quality and standards-based learning. They also require quality digital content, as the process of digitizing materials has been slower than expected.[5]

- It absolutely imperative that students cull the essential, meaningful and reliable data. They must therefore establish criteria for reliability in order to separate the 'wheat from the chaff'. Key action verbs are choose, pick, select, separate, sift, single out.[6]
- Jamie McKenzie tells us also that we should learn to navigate in the mud. *When sailors misread the ebbing tide, they may feel the sudden resistance of soft, sucking mud. The Internet offers its own information mudflats – vast expanses of soft data and opinion that can bog us down and slow our search for truth. Students must learn to skirt these shoals unless they are prepared to dig deeply and carefully.*[7]
- Many schools and most public libraries appear to be blessed with a reliable network. If you are in a school where the network is flaky or locked down by nervous administrators to such an extent that even the most innocuous search is blocked, don't waste your time. Until your school has a system manager capable of building a reliable system, stick to books or direct students to a public internet facility. Above all, don't dissipate the valuable learning time of a class unless you are sure that they will be able to quickly access the web sites you have given them to search.

Practical tips for productive Web searching

- Before students go to the Web, get them to establish a document into which they can place the information they find. They can then select on the run, cut the relevant words, phrases or paragraphs and have somewhere ready to paste them. Also show them how to keep the Web address and the date accessed, ready for final referencing.
- If students have their own laptops, be sure that they have their 'Favourites' folder organised and ready to save the addresses of useful web sites that they find. If, for example, you know they will be doing newspaper searching, there should be a 'drawer' in the 'Favourites' filing cabinet ready to take the Web address when a useful one is found. It will save a lot of effort next time round.
- When you want students to go to a particular web site, give them the address electronically if that is at all possible. A slash facing the wrong way or a misplaced comma means that the address won't work and students are notoriously inaccurate at copying correctly off the blackboard or a printed page.
- Make Web searching a collaborative activity. A lot of good discussion can be generated around a computer screen. It lends itself very well to a group activity so don't be misled by the myth that computers are an isolating way of working.

- Make Web searching fun. Try bringing into the class a packet of Smarties and give one the first student to find the answer to a Trivial Pursuit quiz. Questions could range from 'Who played Nicholas in the recent BBC version of *Nicholas Nickleby*?' to 'What is the topic of today's editorial in the *Straits Times* newspaper in Singapore?' or 'What is the predominant colour that Baz Luhrman uses for the Capulet family in his film version of *Romeo and Juliet*?'. Even: 'Where and when did the poet Sylvia Plath die?' or 'What is the title of David Guterson's most recent novel?'. Follow this up by discussing the path the winners used to find the information first and what steps they went through.

- Have students save the passwords of the school's library subscription services. It should be as easy for a student to go to the *Encyclopaedia Britannica* online in class or at home as it is for them to pull a book off the shelf in the library. If necessary, encourage your librarians to release the resources by making the web sites and passwords readily available and don't be afraid to check that students have these saved for future use.

- Teach footnoting and reference skills so that it is clear how we expect a student to acknowledge sources. Tell them that it is OK to copy from books or web sites. We have all done it. What is not OK is to pretend that it is all our own work and not give the source proper acknowledgment.

- Limit the size of the response in order to force the sifting, culling, choosing and selecting from a mass of data. If, for example, you require a research report by a Year 9 class on the nature of Elizabethan theatre, set a word limit. The rubric could be

Present a report on ... The report must include a maximum of 300 words, one graphic image and a link to one live web site. Direct quotes must be in quotation marks and all sources clearly footnoted. The report must be laid out on one A4 page.

- Each search engine has a Help menu to guide users through its particular style and syntax. Direct students to these and encourage them to use the search tools as the designers intended.

Web sites – resources for thinking

Web sites can be transient, so the recommendation of certain web sites in the following pages is made with some qualification. This is only a very small sample. It is best to build up your own list with colleagues. Like a good reference book, a good web site is like gold, so value it, save it and pass it on to your faculty. If some of the web sites on the following pages are no longer available, just accept such transience as part of the new blueprint for learning.

Sites for pictures

For brilliant pictures that could illustrate responses to poetry or form the basis for a piece or writing, or illustrate a concept in Geography or act as a background for a report in History, try:

http://australiasevereweather.com/

For a searchable index of many thousands of pictures go to the Fine Arts Museum of San Francisco where there are 82,000 images arranged under subject headings:

> http://www.famsf.org/
> or   http://www.ditto.com

Australian pictures from the National Library, the Australian War Memorial, the National Archives, Fryer Library of University of Queensland and the State Libraries of Victoria, Tasmania and New South Wales and many more are all on one web site:

http://www.pictureaustralia.org/

There is also a web site for all of the Australian museums – lots for the students to find in what is called the gateway to the museums and galleries:

http://amol.org.au/discovernet/

Or try copyright-friendly pictures for education arranged under categories at

http://pics.tech4learning.com/

Try http://au.altavista.com/image/ default for the Alta Vista images site. Students could put a word like mystery or danger in the search tool and see what comes up. This is a great way to confront a blank page when you start a piece of creative writing.

Newspapers online

Newspaper study is one of the most valuable student activities online, holds the student's interest and has an immediacy that makes it an effective learning tool. See also Chapter 4, Responding to newspaper issues.

Have a look at the *New York Times* site designed specifically for students. http://www.nytimes.com/learning/

Another way of teaching from newspapers is to discuss a cartoonist's take on a current issue – see http://cagle.slate.msn.com/ for US current cartoons.

Try the cartoon section of the *New York Times*: http://www.nytimes.com/ pages/cartoons/index.html

You will cheer yourself up and your students with a good cartoon such as Randy Glassbergen's Teen Cartoons at:

http://www.borg.com/~rjgtoons/ teen.html

or Jerry King's cartoons at http://www.jerryking.com/

Shakespeare online

A good resource for lesson plans and information about Shakespeare is the Folger Library, which calls itself the 'world's most significant repository of Shakespeare material. Look for it at http: //www.folger.edu/education/teaching.htm

Try taking a virtual tour of the Globe Theatre at http://www.shakespeares-globe.org/

Another site with everything you ever wanted to know about Shakespeare and

an online copy of the scripts, try
http://shakespeare.palomar.edu/

For free electronic books, including
the complete works of Shakespeare,
go to Project Gutenberg at
http://www.gutenberg.net/index.shtml

Online resources for English

Try subscribing to this weekly resource
from New Zealand by getting it for a few
weeks as you decide whether it is worth
continuing:

http://english.unitecnology.ac.nz

The Learning Federation web site is
run by the Australian Commonwealth
Government. At the time of writing
the site was still under development,
but have a look at it to see if there is
something which you can use.

http://www.thelearningfederation.edu.
au/tlf/

The online journal *From Now On* by
Jamie McKenzie is free and excellent for
practical ideas to integrate computers
into learning.

http://fno.org/

Another useful web site which may
be worth a look but you will need to
subscribe to get the full benefit:

http://www.teachit.co.uk/

If you have colleagues or students
who debate matters of style, direct them
to http://www.bartleby.com/141/ The
web site says of itself that it will provide
suggestions to 'avoid tame, colourless,
hesitating, non-committal language'.

Check out Spark Notes -- American
oriented but good teaching material on

almost every text we are likely to teach,
all arranged alphabetically with infinite
numbers of worksheets:

http://www.sparknotes.com/lit/

For papers relating to IT in education
across a global scenario, have a look at
http://www.globaled.com/ and subscribe
to this free service which styles itself as
a peer-reviewed collection of extensive
articles for the global educator.

Look at http://www.dictionarylink.com
It provides a compilation of free online
dictionaries, thesaurus, language
translators, encyclopaedias, crossword
solvers, quotes and other language
resources. It also contains an alternate
page with links to major news sources
and newspapers.

The visual thesaurus, where words
keep popping up around the key word
like satellites around the moon, is great
fun for teachers and students:

http://www.visualthesaurus.com/
online/

Web sites for poetry

Have a look at a poetry web site. There
are plenty around. Here is one to start
with, probably best for upper primary or
lower secondary classes with cool poems
and funny poems and poetry lessons all
laid out for you:

http://www.poetry4kids.com/

If you want to hear authors reading
their poetry to you, go to a site that
offers 'literary audio':

http://www.epc.buffalo.edu/sound/
links.html

Web sites for fiction

Here is the web site of the International Reading Association
http://www.readingonline.org/

There are some good reviews and teaching ideas for American novels and other useful information at the National Council for the Teaching of English (USA) home page at
http://www.ncte.org/

Have you tried to buy a book from the world's biggest online book store? They have great book reviews that are brief and accessible. Students really enjoy finding reviews of books they are reading. It is worth a look …
http://www.amazon.com

As an example of an author's web site, try the Roald Dahl web site with the Quentin Blake illustrations and everything you ever wanted to know about him:
http://www.roalddahl.com

Most authors have their own web site and students seem to enjoy reading the biographical information and other details about an author they have got to know through the printed page.

A few examples of the web sites of authors are

John Marsden
http://www.panmacmillan.com.au/johnmarsden/index.htm

James Moloney
http://www.home.gil.com.au/~cbcqld/james.htm

Libby Hathorn
http://www.libbyhathorn.com

The web site 'Focus on Fiction' offers information about authors and books, all pitched for secondary students:
http://www.eddept.wa.edu.au/cmis/eval/fiction/index.htm

The Young Australia Readers Awards is pitched at upper primary/lower secondary and worth a look:
http://www.yara-online.org

'Magpies' is a great resource for children's and youth literature.
http://www.magpies.net.au/

Try 'Stories from the Web' – there seems to be a range of resources for 11–14-year-olds:
http://www.storiesfromtheweb.org/sfwhomepage.htm

Try this US site for study notes of 375 books – print on screen – but worth a browse if you want more worksheets:
http://www.pinkmonkey.com/

The selection of web sites is a very personal matter. These are some that an English faculty has found useful and bookmarked in the 'Favourites' folders. One measure of collegiality in any faculty will be the extent to which resources, print or online, are shared and made available to colleagues.

Wider applications and suggested activities

In the last few years a whole new world of resources has opened up to everyone that is up-to-date, visually interesting and reliable if you carefully check the source. Should an Economics teacher rely on a text book that is several years old when today's statistics are available from the Treasury, the Bureau of Statistics or the Bureau of Trade?

Of course, library books and text books should not be discarded, but we must acknowledge that there is now a whole new array of Web resources to add to the collection. And as we have said many times, this is an overwhelming task if you are trying to do it on your own. It is absolutely imperative to build up a community of practice and foster a collaborative culture that will not only minimise frustration but lead to some exciting new initiatives.

This can be all so open-ended, but in the best-case scenario will help equip our young people to think for themselves and make up their own minds. This may depend on the kinds of questions we get them to ask and the evidence we require to support their contention. At his seminars, Jamie McKenzie often reminds his audience that questions are the most powerful technology of all.[8] He gives the example of challenging his students before they begin online research studying the early explorers, where he asks them to say which kind of captain they would most like to sail

with – one who is honest or courageous or resourceful or a good navigator or a good manager of people. Once the students have rated these qualities in order of importance as they see them, they are in a better position to evaluate the information they uncover about the various captains they are studying.

The availability of Web resources that are so immediate allow us to seize the moment in quite a dramatic way. For example, around Easter 2004 when Mel Gibson's film *The Passion of the Christ* was getting saturation distribution and was a frequent topic of conversation, one teacher of Religious Education in a laptop class was able to capture the interest of the moment by getting his students to find the web site for the film, read the reviews and then watch online images and the trailers of some of the key scenes. These made a very pertinent and immediate talking point.

Open-ended learning modules

One excellent commercial resource is SchoolKiT,[9] which is accessed online and enables the teacher to browse, select and download hundreds of learning modules across the Arts, Mathematics, Science, Social Studies, English and cross-curricular activities. Modules are organised under subjects and year levels. For example, for Years 9 or 10 you might choose modules on how to write an argumentative essay, how to prepare and present an oral report on a wide-reading book, how to write your own news story, or use a template to gain an overview of a novel by examining the major conflicts in the story. Another offers basic instruction in the use of reason, authority and emotion in development of a piece of persuasive writing. In a Geography class, students could plot the course of an actual cargo ship in live time as it crosses the Atlantic and while doing so, make all sorts of observations about speed, weather danger and the like.

For further details go to the EDclass web site http://www.edclass.com

Write a poem with a poetry slide show

As an example, here is the first page of the module on how to write a poem and prepare a poetry slide show for the following lesson:

Challenge

You are going to make a poetry show. You will:

▶ create a slide master with a photograph on it;

▶ make a slide and multiple copies of it;

▶ write a poem, typing one phrase on each slide; and

▶ set up a slide show to present your poem.

I know a place where a steely river streams silently into the distance,

I know a place

To help you understand the project you are going to look at a sarr show.

▶ Before you click the button to view the project, read these instructions

• When the slide show is finished, click to use it

• Restore the resource sheet

A sample project

▶ To start the **Project sample**, click this button then minimise the sheet

Project sample

A class was given this to do as a homework activity. The sets of slides which the students showed each other included the two below. They are nothing profound, but for boys who wouldn't previously involve themselves with poetry it was quite a breakthrough:

We scurry about thinking we're making a difference contributing money to Green Peace

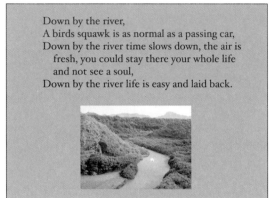

Down by the river,
A birds squawk is as normal as a passing car,
Down by the river time slows down, the air is
    fresh, you could stay there your whole life
    and not see a soul,
Down by the river life is easy and laid back.

Endnotes

[1] V. Watson & M. Kairouz, 'Student learning and information processing in the knowledge age: a case for the strategic teaching of thinking skills'. IARTV Occasional Paper, No 75, May 2002.

[2] J. O'Donoghue, 'To cope, to contribute, to control', in A. Goodwyn (ed.), *English in the digital age: information and communications technology and the teaching of English*, Cassell, 2000, p. 72.

[3] B. Schneiderman, *Leonardo's laptop: human needs and the new computing technologies*, MIT Press, Cambridge, Massachusetts, 2003, p. 123.

[4] M. Kennedy & M. Lee-Ack, 'Review: Net texts: exploring electronic English', *English in Australia*, journal of the Australian Association for the Teaching of English, No. 137, Winter 2003.

[5] *From Now On: The Educational Technology Journal*, Vol. 12, No. 11, Summer 2003, viewed 10 May 2004, <http://www.fno.org/sum03/nowwhat.html>

[6] J. McKenzie, 1999, *How teachers learn technology best*, FNO Press, 1999, p. 51.

[7] ibid., p. 52.

[8] J. McKenzie, 'We've done the Internet. Now what?' Speech presented at a seminar in Melbourne 28/02/04. Viewed 10 May 2004, <http://www.fno.org/sum03/nowwhat.html>

[9] The author has used a number of SchoolKiT modules in the classroom to supplement and extend the student's activities. See Appendix 2 for further information.

Chapter 10

'In times of radical change, the learners inherit the earth, while the learned find themselves perfectly equipped for a world that no longer exists.'[1]

Responding to student work:

Can computers help?

The learning and thinking context

Even the most enthusiastic and experienced teachers who have sharp antennas for the valid learning experiences of children and are keen to allow computers to enrich the constructivist learning goals in their classroom, still find many practical difficulties with this new medium. Change is at best incremental rather than revolutionary; risk-taking can be challenging and draining, and the practical support and understanding of colleagues is vital. We all struggle with the demands of planning, class management, the changing and more fragile social situation of many children and the effects that all this has on learning. Now add to this the seemingly endless corrections and we may well wonder where computers fit into the picture, if at all.

If computers are going to be more to us than a glorified typewriter, we will need to think differently about the nature of teaching and learning. One consequence is that we also need to think differently about how students respond, how they submit their responses and how we as teachers give feedback.

Andrew Goodwyn says
[of all the] activities that dominate English teachers' time none is so relentless as marking, the physical act of putting marks on student's work ... yet most teachers frequently doubt that their efforts are making the difference that they hope to achieve ... If [however,] the student completes a truly provisional electronic text, then the teacher has far more options.[2]

Computers hit classrooms in the early 1980s, at about the same time as the process writing movement associated so strongly with the name of Donald Graves. In many ways the two thrusts complemented each other. It was a hassle for students to redraft or even make simple corrections when these had to be done in longhand, so only the most diligent were willing to take this burden seriously. The new digital medium has enabled us to allow students to walk away from a text and return to develop it at a later stage with little effort required in the process. There is more chance now that the final version will have had some mature reflection and genuine reconstruction, if it is required.

Yes, they do still need at times to write under pressure in a formal written examination and this kind of writing will still need some practice. The inherent motivation, however, of getting a good mark in an examination has to be balanced against

> *[the] intrinsic motivation that comes from a writer having something to say and also the conviction that 'saying it the right way' will take time and effort. A great deal of writing under pressure is forced, inaccurate and inadequate. In the educational attempt to balance such pressure, teachers will find that technology gives them far greater flexibility, so they can make the most of this potential in the way they support and monitor a student's development as a writer ... Equally with the texts such as the essay, ... teachers and students have far more opportunity to 'play with' the logic and emotional structures of their compositions, with the teacher having several opportunities to assist the writer with suggestions, corrections and additional ideas.[3]*

So often we feel good about putting red marks on a page, finding some grammatical errors and thinking that we are helping the learning of a child. In fact, if we are honest, we will admit that many students rushed the original work, ignore our painstaking comments, knew the correct spelling and syntax anyway but could not be bothered to proofread the original, and were interested only in the grade. Will computers make any difference to this situation or are they just another chore, another complication to add to our already busy lives?

Classroom strategies

In this chapter, we will explore some suggestions that will hopefully make life easier, not more complex, in this new teaching and learning environment.

Keep your eye on the big picture

One of the huge advantages of computers in any subject is that they make it easy for a piece of work to be revisited, redrafted and revised with relative ease. Rather than focusing on the important yet somewhat trivial aspects of spelling and syntax, most of which could be dealt with by spelling and grammar-checking software, word processing of comments now allows the student and teacher to stand back and view the piece from a distance.

Several years ago at a school camp, a bored student too sick to join in a climbing activity, asked if he could read a paper I was preparing for a forthcoming 'Computers in Education' conference. I anticipated no more than a casual glance at my computer screen while I went to get a coffee. Instead, when I came back, I found that he had used the 'Add Comment' function in Word to make genuinely global observations, indicating to me that he had tried to come to terms with the ideas I was grappling with in the paper. He wrote in various places:

- The paper has a reasonably strong focus on the point of making education a better and more open experience. Examples are good but the examples don't completely speak for themselves and need to be clarified – exactly what is what that the teachers were trying to get out of it. What you might also consider in this first half is how the technology affects the teachers' own widened concepts of reaching out to the students.

- I think this should be extended as it is a highly important issue in terms of not opening possibilities but making use of the flexibility available.

- This needs to be explained to a greater extent. Why is having such a live resource so valuable?

- I think a little elaboration is necessary here to recognise the foreign ground that teachers were put on.

Of course, this was an astute senior student and I would not expect that level of perception from most of the students I teach, but it was nevertheless a very valuable model for me, as an example of the ways in which I could be responding myself to student writing. It was also a shock to find a student looking so carefully and critically at my text!

Rather than getting bogged down with the minutiae of spelling and grammatical errors, why not use the Word Add Note function or a Text Box at the end of the document to make global comments which challenge the thinking of the students and help them to reflect on the quality of their learning. There are many friends and family who could help students pick up basic errors if students cannot do this for themselves, quite apart from the spelling and grammar checkers that are now available. Teachers have a much broader role to play in responding to student work.

Play down the routine tasks

Quick tests that indicate homework has been completed or a piece of class teaching understood are important ways for a teacher to monitor the outcomes of teaching and a way of introducing future work. It is easy to get bogged down with the correction of routine work, but more time spent in careful preparation could save hours of marking. Perhaps this kind of work could be marked by the students themselves or by exchanging computers or by the teacher marking while the work is being done. We are all guilty of setting a piece of writing on the spur of the moment as a class management activity, only to find that because we did not define the rubric carefully or have a clear idea of the purpose of the task, we are left with hours of pointless corrections.

For example, we could set an essay asking students to summarise the main ideas and characters in an act of a play. Alternatively, we could select text from the Web and use the Table/Insert function of Word to set up a homework exercise. Here is one on Act III of *The Merchant of Venice*:

The text	Who is speaking? To whom? Where is the scene set?	What is the context? What has just happened? What happens next?	Summarise the meaning. Explain why these lines are important.
Act 3, Scene 1, line 37 He was wont to call me usurer; let him look to his bond.			
Act 3, Scene 2, line 310 Come, away; For you shall hence upon your wedding day.			
Act 3, Scene 3, line 26 The Duke cannot deny the course of law.			

There are some good commercial programs for setting multiple choice or one-word answer tests, and many of these are self-correcting. The danger is that they may be costly to purchase and once understood and set up, the teacher may be tempted to re-use the test and so lose the freshness of quickly responding to the interests of a particular class.

One very easy-to-use product that is free, with certain conditions, is Hot Potatoes.[4] It has the facility for designing multiple choice questions, which Science teachers love so much; short-answer questions, which are useful in any Humanities subject; jumbled sentence exercises, crossword puzzles, mix and match exercises and cloze or fill in the blank exercises to test the student's ability to make meaning within a context.

Another even more accessible option is to use the Forms toolbar in Word. With this facility, it is possible to construct

- **a blank text box** – allowing students to complete sentences, insert words or complete a short answer;
- **a drop-down multiple-choice box** – allowing the teacher to give students a number of choices from which they can pick the correct response;
- **a tick box** – similar to multiple choice except the student ticks the box next to the appropriate answer.

Some tasks do not need to be collected and laboriously marked provided the teacher is active in watching and responding to the work as the students are doing it. Self-correction or peer assessments are also good ways of dealing quickly with some responses.

Plan the method of submission when you plan the task

We can no longer stand at the door and collect the written homework when students are working onscreen, so the careful planning of the method of submission becomes even more important. Some teachers like working with e-mail attachments, while others find this clunky and time-consuming. Collecting discs is clumsy and may open the door to viruses if students do not keep the virus checker up-to-date on their home computer. Plugging the teacher's memory stick into the USB port of each student's computer is an effective way to collect work but can be a lengthy process. Students with a laptop can 'infra-red' their files to the teacher, but only one at a time.

Many teachers find that a 'common drive' or 'drop box' on the school's network is the most efficient way to gather student work, and perhaps the only way if the student has hyperlinked documents behind the main piece of writing. It may also be necessary when dealing with Inspiration documents which don't attach to e-mail in some systems. This drop box works best if the teacher can see work from every student, open it, correct it and return it, while the student can only see their own work. The teacher can then tell students when to retrieve the corrected work and save it back to their own storage space.

One major problem with this method of submission is that teachers may have to do all their marking at school in order to be online. Of course, this will depend on the helpfulness of the technicians, the efficiency of the school's network and the speed of home access, if that is possible at all.

There is also a need to save teacher frustration and the potential mix-up of computer documents, which all look similar when students forget to put their names on their work. It is good to get students into the habit of putting a header and footer on every document. The header could include student name, subject and class, while the footer would include the topic, teacher's name and date. It will save time if a blank document is set up with the header and footer in place and saved as a template ready for future re-use.

Computers as a personal workspace

This is one of the strongest arguments for laptops or one-to-one computing. We all possess some degree of fussiness when it comes to our study desk with preferred pens and pencils, paper, envelopes, scissors, eraser and suchlike. Using a computer that is not our own is exactly the same as going to someone else's desk and finding things organised differently – fonts, toolbars and other features have all been customised to the preferences of another person.

Some teachers like to keep electronic copies of all student work because it is so easy to do, yet generally in the past we did not keep photocopies of student written work. The exception may be special examples to show at a parent–teacher interview, hopefully conducted

at a place where we are online. However, it is important to ensure that students themselves keep all original and corrected versions of tasks. Just as in the past we would get them to label their folders for the subject with tabs such as poetry/novel/folio/oral, etc, so now folders can be set up at the start of the year in *My Documents* so that even the most messy students can save and subsequently find their work. Boys in particular comment on the advantages of computers for this kind of organisation and storage.

In a survey conducted in 2001 on the use of laptop computers,[5] it was found that if computers really are to be a personal workspace, then most work must be done on them, at least in the lower and middle secondary years. Why do we need to burden students with the weight and hassle of both a paper and an electronic system? The data collected showed that computers are mainly used for research and responses other than traditional essays at the lower and middle secondary levels. If there is an immersion in this digital technology for a range of classroom activities in say Years 7 to 10, students in the later years will choose for themselves the most comfortable learning style and means of response with or without computers. However, they must have the skills and experience if it is to be an informed choice, and most now come from primary schools with very advanced IT skills.

Classroom management

There is the ever-present issue of classroom management[6] and control when students have a very tempting toy in front of them, especially if they know more about the tricks of using it than their teachers. Also, some of us seem to think that we can ask students to open paper folders for us to check but that laptops are somehow private and personal, and teachers should not probe what students do with their computers or how they file their work.

A simple trick to add to the repertoire of steps used to keep one step ahead of the students is to use the Alt/Tab function on a student's keyboard to quickly see what applications are open.

Cheating will always be an issue in schools, as it is in universities. Now it is easier than ever to copy documents and swap homework, but all of this is still a discipline issue and teachers will have to deal with it in the same ways that they have always done with misbehaviour. In this, as in online tests and examinations, it is more important than ever before that teachers set tasks requiring higher-order thinking skills rather than factual recall. In the case of an online examination, there is no point in asking questions if the answers can be sourced from the data on their own computer, just as open-book examinations test understanding rather than the facts in the book taken into the examination room. The students interviewed in the survey above did not believe that cheating was any more of an issue than in the past.[7]

Students can be critical of teachers who prepare electronic worksheets and require online classwork submission, then print out the responses presumably because they are not comfortable correcting it electronically. Some students, who don't like computers, think that it is a lot easier to have everything on paper but plead that teachers should at least stick to one thing or the other. One said, 'We get confused if there is occasional use of computers, then we have to keep paper files as well'. Another asked, 'If they give you a laptop, why do they then give out worksheets as well?' One Year 11 student got around this by throwing away every piece of paper, except the few really vital ones which he stuffed in his laptop bag. This is one method of coping with a practical problem!

Wider applications and suggested activities

Computers can save an enormous amount of marking time. The many **advantages** include:

- a definite record of work submission, date and time;
- no papers piled up on your desk;
- reduced risk of misplacing work;
- work comments and corrections that are easily retained if required, allowing comparison with future work submissions or a record for parent–teacher interviews;
- easy onscreen correction mode.

There are, however, significant **disadvantages**, including:

- tedious onscreen correction if this means long periods in front of the computer screen;
- that students sometimes don't read comments placed in an electronic file just as they may not have read the comments on paper;
- the need for students to have access to an e-mail account and if they are working from home, they may not want to mix school work with their Hotmail account;
- problems with student access to the network in some schools.

Experiment with e-correction

The actual process of e-correction can be very easy once you have good typing abilities and have established a routine.

It is a good idea to first set up some e-mail filters that allow you to segregate students' submissions from everyday e-mails. This will ensure that your inbox does not become clogged and difficult to navigate.

A good way of putting in shortcuts is via Tools/Auto correct where you can choose the colour and size. You could, for example, put in 'sy' as the abbreviation and a smiley ☺ as the text.

Some personal abbreviations could be:

sx = Correct the syntax of this sentence

pa = Paragraph structure needs attention

sp = Check spelling and proofread before submission

rp = You are repeating the same phrase or words

hf = Put in the correct header and footer

pn = Punctuation needs attention

aw = Awkward expression – check this sentence

bd = Poor choice of words – broaden your vocabulary

sy = ☺

z = ☑

zx = ☒

Another way of doing this is to go to Insert/Symbols/Wingdings2.

Select a tick ✓ and assign a shortcut to it such as Ctrl F1.

Every time you now put your cursor at a certain place in a document and press Ctrl F1, a tick will be put in that place.

Choose another symbol such as a cross ✘ or a smiley ☺ or a star ★ or a sports ⚲ symbol, or whatever else you may want to use, and assign a shortcut to it. Have a play. Remember what you have assigned as the shortcut keys.

If you are making comments electronically, it is a good idea to have your name on the comment. To ensure this happens, go to *Word/Tools/Options/User Information* and insert your name and initials, but only if you always use the same computer. Your name will appear on the student work you correct electronically. Similarly, students who work on their own computers and exchange work or send work to a teacher annotated with comments from the reviewing tool bar will have their name on the comment if they have personalised their user information.

If you are using Outlook, go to *Outlook/Tools/Options* when the Inbox is open, and tick the box 'Use Word as you e-mail editor'. This will ensure that the features you are used to in Word will be there on your screen when you use e-mail.

We are all breaking new ground in the area of computers and learning. While it has always been important to ask students to evaluate and reflect on their learning, it seems even more important now.

Students in one class were asked for a review and evaluation of their classroom work and comments on how their learning had changed since the introduction of laptops. While some students felt insecure in the more open-ended learning environment, the following comments were encouraging:

I learned more about myself and I tried things that I wouldn't normally try. These tasks have really opened my mind and made me more interested in English.

The modules we did helped me and kept me busy, let me tell you that much! I found that it was a very good way to present work to students such as me, and you could always find extra work to do in these modules. The work was to a certain extent, endless.

I enjoyed this semester of English. It was a much easier way to work because you can do some whenever you have spare time rather than having to rush homework because you have to go to sport or work. I thought my personal strengths were Creative Writing and Interpreting Current World Issues. I also thought my poetry improved throughout the year and I can interpret poetry better. I enjoyed the class discussions when talking about world issues. I would have enjoyed it if we had more of these.

I learnt from this module that I have amazing levels of untapped creative wells that I did not even know about.

What more could a teacher ask?

Endnotes

[1] Eric Hoffer, quoted in I. Jukes, 'Digital kids: learning in a new landscape', viewed 1 December 2004, <http://www.lasb.com/files/j4030407.htm>

[2] A. Goodwyn (ed.), *English in the digital age: information and communications technology and the teaching of English*, Cassell, London, 2000, p. 13.

[3] ibid., p. 14.

[4] 'Hot Potatoes', viewed 26 January 2005, <http://web.uvic.ca/hrd/halfbaked/> For further details see p. 158.

[5] D. Nettelbeck, 'Computers and learning: does ICT really change the way secondary English students learn?' *English in Australia*, No. 134, journal of the Australian Association for the Teaching of English, July 2002, p. 78.

[6] These issues are dealt with more fully in Chapter 1.

[7] D. Nettelbeck, 2002, op. cit., p. 83.

Chapter 11

'Never before has it been more necessary that people learn how to read, write, and think critically. It's not just point and click.

It's point, read, think, click.'[1]

Whole brain learning, whole brain assessment:

Exemplar units for English and History

**Whole brain learning,
whole brain assessment:
Exemplar units for
English and History**

The learning and thinking context

Melbourne teacher, innovator and entrepreneur Bruce Dixon realised more than 20 years ago that computers allowed children to do things that were not possible with pen and paper: 'The whole idea of giving them different learning experiences that identified skills that we couldn't otherwise see was part of my growing awareness'.[2] Amid the excitement of bits and bytes, Bruce saw beyond the simple issues of adequate connectivity and access, to the changing social experiences of children and the changing nature of learning in the 21st-century classroom.

In the 1990s, the digital divide was characterized as a gap in technology access that translated into inequities in educational, economic, social, and civic opportunities among sectors of the population. Since then, education leaders have come to realize that access is simply the first step. Equally important are robust home access and the readiness of individuals to use technology, communication networks, and information efficiently, effectively, and productively … It's time for the education of our children to shift from plateaus of knowing to continuous cycles of learning.[3]

One of the first laptop teachers at MLC in Melbourne, Adam Smith, similarly realised the potential of this new kind of learning when the school pioneered the introduction of laptop computers. He observed that in this new, constructivist-style classroom, 'relatively young kids were spending more of their time working things out for themselves, or in collaboration with their peers … we provided a scaffold but the kids built their buildings, and each was different.[4]

This kind of teaching for better thinking owes a lot to Piaget, who saw children not so much as empty vessels to be filled but active builders of knowledge. The quest for understanding is at the core of any kind of constructivist educational enterprise where teachers seek and value students' points of view, challenge suppositions, pose problems and structure learning around 'big' concepts and ideas. This is a theme that has been developed throughout this book.

The Writing Reading Assessment Project (WRAP) revealed that between 1989 and 1991, 75 per cent of all Year 10 writing tasks in South Australia allowed students no choice in any aspect of the task and only 1 per cent allowed students choice in purpose, audience or form.[5] Many teachers are well aware of situations similar to this.

What steps, therefore, can we take to encourage individuals to use their preferred intelligences in learning, to deliberately appeal in our teaching activities to different forms of intelligence, build in real choice and take account of multiple forms of intelligence when we assess work?

Classroom strategies

The following units of work make some attempt to build on the theory outlined above. They do not set out to make use of computers as though we have to find artificial ways of justifying the expense. Instead, it is assumed that one-to-one computing, or other generous provisions for connectivity, is available as a seamless element of the teaching and learning environment, and that given the choice, students will opt for the tools appropriate to their preferred learning style and the nature of the task they have chosen.

The novel *Holes* – a Year 8 or 9 text study

Holes, by Louis Sachar, was first published in the United States in 1998, in Britain in 2000, and has become very popular as a class text in Australian schools in the last few years. In 2003,

Disney released a highly praised film version of the novel for which the author was also the screenwriter. It is an enigmatic and multi-layered story that has spawned an abundance of teacher resources, mostly available on the Web. These are generally well constructed and are sincerely intentioned, screen-delivered worksheets. Most are just text on screen with a little more colour and movement than you might find on a printed page. They follow the predictable formula of 'fill in the blanks' or 'answer the question by guessing what is in the teacher's mind'. These may be useful in some way and will certainly be a good starting point for busy teachers. But where are the unrestricted, mind-challenging tasks to stimulate and encourage thinking? We are making no pretence to succeed where others may not have done so, but the following is an attempt at more open-ended tasks which build in a great deal of choice for the students.

**Whole brain learning,
whole brain assessment:
Exemplar units for
English and History**

An open-ended research task

- *Choose ANY TOPIC related to the **background or setting** of this novel.*
- ***Research** your topic through the Web or from printed library resources.*
- *Prepare a **report** with careful attention to a heading, graphics and layout.*
- *Your report will be **presented** in Publisher or Word and include the following:*
  - *Approximately 200–300 words of text*
  - *Clear quotation marks where you have copied material PLUS an acknowledgement of your sources*
  - *A picture or graphic or drawing*
  - *A link to a web site.*

Some possible topics for research
- *The life, background and other books by the author*
- *Juvenile justice in this state*
- *Juvenile justice in Texas*
- *Water conservation*
- *The yellow spotted lizard*
- *Rattlesnakes*
- *Scorpions*
- *Recipe for spiced peaches*
- *Family migration*
- *Digging up the past*
- *Any relevant topic which interests you*

Remember that a good report will include
- clear headings and subheadings;
- well laid-out text with clear sentence and paragraphs breaks;
- an annotated bibliography;
- annotations to explain the illustrations;
- pictures and graphics;
- links to web sites.

Theme study and oral – a wide choice of response options

- While this is an enjoyable story, Sachar also deals with significant **themes** or **issues** in the course of this novel.
- In a group of two or three, choose any **ONE of the themes** below or any other theme that you think is significant. Be sure that each group in the class chooses a different theme to explore.
- You may **explore this theme** in any way you wish, so long as you relate it to very **specific** incidents and characters in the novel. Look for patterns, opposites, reversals, conflicts and chain reactions as you trace your theme.
- You may **summarise** your understandings of the theme in a **Word document** using AutoShapes/ Connectors OR in maximum of six PowerPoint slides *with a maximum of six dot points per slide and a maximum of six words per dot point OR you may find it easiest to use an* **Inspiration map**, *OR use the* **Diagram Gallery** *from the Drawing Toolbar in Word XP.*
- *Your teacher will arrange a time for you to* **present your findings** *to the class or to a group within the class.*

Some suggested themes to explore

Family	Destiny
Race	Bullying
Alienation	Loyalty
Optimism	Perseverance
Ancestral identity	Friendship
Power	Justice
Relationships	Courage
Survival	Kindness
Brutality	Any other theme

Character analysis using concept-mapping software

- Use **Inspiration** to prepare a character map. It is best to design your own map but you may get ideas from Inspiration/File/ Template/Character or Comparison or Literary Web where basic maps are done for you to adapt and use, if you wish to do so.
- Choose any **TWO significant characters from the novel**. Put them into TWO MAIN boxes.
- Now put in other boxes which show other characters who relate to your two main characters. You should choose at least half of the characters from the list below.
- It is essential that you **name the links** to show the relationships between the characters.
- Now in an **Add Notes** box behind each character, record notable personality traits (influential, conceited, hateful, etc.) and at least TWO incidents from the novel where these traits are evident.
- **Submit** your character map by saving to the H Drive on the date and with the file name which your teacher will give you.

Whole brain learning,
whole brain assessment:
Examplar units for
English and History

Character list

Stanley Yelnats	Zero
X Ray	Squid
Magnet	Armpit
Zigzag	Warden
Charles Walker	Sam
Elya Yelnats	Madam Zeroni
Stanley Yelnats I	Mrs Yelnats
Mr Sir	Mr Yelnats
Mr Pendanski	Clyde
Livingstone	Derrick Dunne

Vocabulary and word study task

- Find the word in the text and study exactly the way it is used by the author.
- Look up the word in a dictionary and/or a thesaurus. Study the meaning.
- Complete the table below.

Key word	Meaning	Metaphorical or special use of the word in the novel
shrivelled (3)		
stifling (6)		
pretend (7)		
barren (11)		
destiny (24)		
despicable (25)		
wreck (43)		
delirious (128)		
mirage (152)		
moon (153, 161)		
shadow (166)		
fugitive (188)		

Creative writing – a traditional essay enhanced by pictures or hyperlinks

- *Choose any ONE of the sentences below.*
- *Use the sentence as an idea or starting point for a personal or creative piece of writing.*
- *You DO NOT need to use the ideas from the novel or write about the novel. Just write your OWN true or imaginary story.*

'... and just a little bit of luck.' (8)

'If only, if only ...' (9)

'This isn't a Girl Scout camp.' (14)

'Nobody believed him when he said he was innocent.' (22)

'You don't need a lawyer ... just tell the truth.' (25)

'They did it to "build character".' (71)

'He was staring very intently at the busted television screen.' (73)

'He was in the wrong place at the wrong time.' (85)

'The last thing we need is an investigation.' (139)

'Who will dig the grave for me?' (162)

'We're almost there.' (167)

Wide reading response

It is a common practice for teachers to ask students to write a book report as one accountability measure after a wide reading assignment. Students often find these essays boring to write as it can be a difficult format in which to express their enthusiasm or other feelings for what was hopefully a moving piece of fiction.

The following more open-ended format may stimulate the interest of the students:[6]

After reading your chosen book, you will be asked to prepare a report. It will contain the usual context of:

- *Title*
- *Author*
- *Genre, fiction, non-fiction, etc*
- *Date started, date finished*
- *Brief statement of the time and setting of the book.*

*The major part of your report will be under the heading **My interaction with the book**.*

*For this, you will choose **ANY** of the suggestions below OR make up a topic of your own.*

Your response will include the following:

- *Between **300 and 400 words of text***
- *At least one **image or graphic** relevant to the response*
- *At least one **live hyperlink** to a web site related to the author, publisher, place or theme of the book.*

Here are some suggestions for your interaction with the text :

1 **Unanswered questions** *– e.g. Does your book have an 'open ending'? Are you satisfied with this type of ending? What are the unresolved issues? Make some predictions.*
2 **Reading between the lines** *– You may choose to write a more 'traditional' response which shows your ability to analyse a text. In your response you should include a discussion of themes, plot, character, setting and language features.*

Whole brain learning,
whole brain assessment:
Examplar units for
English and History

3 **Advice to the librarians** *about this and other books for the library.*

4 **Alternative ending.** *Write another ending for the story.*

5 **Suggestions about how the characters could have acted differently** *in specific situations and how this may have affected the outcome.*

6 **Real life experiences** *which this book reminded me of.*

7 **Patterns and connections with other books on the same or similar theme.**

8 **What I learnt about human nature** *or moral lessons from this book – about people, relationships and communication. What makes the characters believable or unbelievable?*

9 *'One man's junk is another man's treasure'* – **Search for differing reviews of this book** *and explanation of why I think it has had such a reaction. Why I liked or disliked this book and why someone else may disagree. (Go to the site http://www.amazon.com, or other web sites, to see what other readers have said about it.)*

10 **Let me introduce the author to you** *(Find web sites produced by or about the author. How useful is the site? What have you learned about the author? What has surprised you? What else would you like to know? Research the author's writing context – historical, social, political, ideological etc? E-mail the author and conduct an interview. Prepare a newsletter for a 'fan club'. Conduct an e-mail survey about this author around the class, or among others who have read the book.*

11 **Re-create a scene** *in a maximum of six comic strip frames.*

12 **Sound file** *where you recreate the dialogue between two of the characters at a critical point in the story OR an audio interpretation of the book such as a dramatic reading, a commentary, a review, a debate, an interview.*

13 **Graphic interpretation** *of the book such as a portrait gallery, alternative settings, 'collage', symbolic representation of the main ideas, a series of advertisements, a film poster or a video clip.*

Senior literature text study: *The Lost Salt Gift of Blood*

The Lost Salt Gift of Blood is an anthology of short stories by Alistair McLeod. The novel can be taught in the traditional way, but the response and assessment tasks below are designed to take into account a whole range of interests and thinking skills.

Research report

Prepare a report *on the setting and author for the collection of stories. You may choose to research Nova Scotia, Cape Breton, Gaelic language, Gaelic myths and traditions, the life of Alistair McLeod, the journeys of the characters or any other aspect that may interest you.*

Your report will include:

- *about 300 words of text;*
- *pictures or graphics to illustrate your understanding of the setting and background of the author*
- *some biographical, historical and/or geographical information;*
- *use of direct quotes for any information copied directly from a book or a web site;*
- *acknowledgement of sources in footnotes or a bibliography;*
- *a maximum length of two A4 pages;*
- *carefully considered aspects of layout and design with a format attractive to the reader.*

You may find useful information at the Cape Breton web site:

http://capebretonisland.com/ OR

browse the collection of the Boston Museum of Fine Arts, particularly the Winslow Homer *paintings or others that may relate to the setting of the stories:*

http://www.mfa.org/home.htm

Oral response

One strength of this anthology is in the detail of the description.

Choose ONE sentence *from a story that is different to the one you will use for the subsequent sections.*

Find ONE picture or drawing *that for you illustrates that sentence or assists your understanding of the scene.*

Present the text and the illustration in ONE PowerPoint slide.

Use that slide as a basis for the explanation of what you found

significant in the story, or the way the writer expressed the details or any other aspect that you found significant.

Be prepared to read aloud to the class a section of the story. The reading and your explanation should take between two and three minutes.

In preparing this slide, you may wish to use

- *a search engine to find some work of Winslow Homer OR*
- *go to the San Francisco Museum of Fine Arts with a key word for the search http://www.famsf.org/ OR*
- *the picture site if you know what you are looking for http://pics.tech4learning.com/ OR*
- *the spectacular pictures at the Australian Severe Weather site http://australiasevereweather.com/ OR*
- *the Australian gallery collection at http://www.pictureaustralia.org/ OR*
- *the Boston Museum of Fine Arts http://www.mfa.org/home.htm*

For an example of a student response to this task see page 52.

Annotation of a passage from the text

Choose a passage *of about half a page or about two paragraphs from one story. The passage will be a very clear description for you of a character or animal.*

Put it into your Word Document either

- *by typing it in or*
- *by scanning it in or*
- *by reading it into a sound file.*

Whole brain learning,
whole brain assessment:
Examplar units for
English and History

Now **annotate the passage** with callout boxes or a verbal explanation or in some other way. As you do this, you will be demonstrating why this passage was important to you, in what ways it is typical of Alistair McLeod's writing, in what ways the use of language is significant ... or anything else you would like to say about it.

Your annotation or comment will total approximately 200 to 300 words.

Concept map on the themes of the stories

Your task is to **create a** concept **map using Inspiration**. The aim will be for you to demonstrate your detailed knowledge of the text and your understanding of the links between some of the elements in the stories.

Choose **one** of the ideas or themes below as your **Main Idea**.

Pain, joy, sacrifice, isolation, tradition, weather, family, animals and people, death, life cycles

1 From the Main Idea, develop at least four links. These could be to a character or theme or symbol or some aspect of the story that you would like to explore.
2 Label the links. This is most important as the link between the central theme and the idea you are exploring will help to clarify your thinking and communicate it to the reader.

3 Write, in either the boxes or as an Add Note, specific details or examples from the text to explain very carefully how the other ideas link to your Main Idea. There will be a total of about 250 to 350 words in all your notes.

Essay response

Write an essay of between 300 and 400 words on any one of the topics below or make up your own topic if there is something you wish to explore.

Your piece must include at least three hyperlinks which could be to images, maps or links to any of the documents above, but there must be no more than one direct link to a live web site and this must be clearly relevant to the argument you are developing.

- 'Cape Breton could be anywhere. It is immediately accessible to us.' Discuss.
- 'Every story is tragic because the characters are not only destined for death but they fail to connect with life while they live.' Do you agree?
- 'Isolation is more than geographical.' Do you agree?
- Are family ties a gift or a curse?
- 'There is no room for love or hope in any story in this collection.' Do you agree?

141

In response to the task of annotating a passage from the text, *The Lost Salt Gift of Blood*, this is the response that one student submitted after selecting for himself the story and passage:

> **Section C – Annotation of a passage - character or animal**
>
> **The Boat**
>
> My mother ran her house as her brothers ran their boats. Everything was clean and spotless and in order. She was tall and dark and powerfully energetic. In later years she reminded me of the women of Thomas Hardy, particularly Eustacia Vye, in a physical way. She fed and clothed a family of seven children, making all of the meals and most of the clothes. She grew miraculous gardens and magnificent flowers and raised broods of hens and ducks. She would walk miles on berry-picking expeditions and hoist her skirts to dig for clams when the tide was low. She was fourteen years younger than my father, whom she had married when she was twenty-six and had been a local beauty for a period of ten years. My mother was of the sea as were all of her people, and her horizons were the very literal ones she scanned with her dark and fearless eyes.

Great description, vintage Alistair McLeod, it's such a good description because she runs it so organised, as if any good boat isn't organised it won't catch many fish.

Uses famous people to relate his descriptions. For example, she moves like Michael Jackson does the moonwalk.

This sentence is very powerful because it explains how the mother thinks and acts, just by explaining her eyes, to me this part of the passage is the most powerful.

Always gives background information about the character to put you into the picture even more.

McLeod always gives a lot of background information on all of his characters; this is a characteristic of his writing.

Very detailed descriptions, it puts the picture straight into your head.

Middle school History unit on World War II

After four weeks of class study, in which many of the tasks below were completed in class or for homework in a quite traditional manner, the following was set as an assessment task:[7]

Prepare an online publication on a significant event for Australia during W.W.II. It will include a front page only and at least four hyperlinks, at least one of which will be to a live web site.

Your front page must include: banner, headline, factual detail of event (who, what, where, when, how and why),

Whole brain learning,
whole brain assessment:
Examplar units for
English and History

*picture, advertisement, and could also
have an 'odd spot' or 'in brief' report.*

*Embedded to any of the above will
be hyperlinks to at least four of the
following:*

- *Cartoon with annotations – use at
  least four callout boxes that explore
  the content and context.*
- *Interview with someone who recalls
  the event and a compilation of their
  reflections, thoughts and feelings of
  the time and experience.*
- *A poem, photograph, artwork,
  music from the time with an
  accompanying personal response.*
- *An editorial from a newspaper of
  the day about the event and a brief
  reflection on the content and tone.*
- *An editorial that you have written
  that reflects the tone, attitude and
  position of the time.*
- *Speech from the time.*
- *Newsreel from the time.*
- *A link to a live web site.*
- *A film that deals with the event
  examined and an annotation of an
  image from the film.*
- *An excerpt from a newsreel of the
  time with a brief written reflection
  of the content and context.*

Students were then given a list of ten
essay topics on which to base the front
page of their newspaper with topics
such as: 'The sinking of HMAS Sydney
1 December 1921 by the German raider
Kormoran off the Western Australian
coast'. The significant element of this
study was that the students were able to
integrate via hypertext many elements of
their classwork into the final one-page
document.

Flanders Fields – a multi-disciplinary unit for Years 8 or 9

This unit attempts to combine the
stimulus of a recently published and
brilliant picture story book, using online
and print resources, the enjoyment we
know students get from writing a picture
story book for a real audience and the
opportunity for some challenging lateral
thinking which incorporates a response
to visual literacy elements. Many
English teachers in Australia normally
include a unit on war around the time
of Anzac Day (25 April), and a unit
on World War I is commonly taught in
History or SOSE (Studies of Society and
Environment) in Years 8 or 9.[8]

The learning goals

- *To examine the ways in which war
  in general is represented from
  multiple perspectives of historians,
  painters, poets, writers and
  participants.*
- *To investigate in detail some
  aspects of World War I.*
- *To read some literature and original
  documents from the period.*
- *To seamlessly integrate traditional
  study and research methods with the
  new literacies now made available
  through the use of information and
  computing technologies.*
- *To introduce students to at least
  three ways of reading a narrative
  about war: as a children's picture
  story book, as an accurate historical
  record and as an insight into the
  lives of participants.*

The starting point

In Flanders Fields *by Norman
Jorgensen and Brian Harrison-Lever.
Published by Sandcastle Books,
August 2003. This book won first
prize in the Australian Children's Book
Council Picture Book Award for 2003.*

As students read this book, they will
be encouraged to respond to their first
impressions by formulating their own
questions and examining such issues as:

- *What were the authors conveying in
  this book?*
- *How effective is this format for that
  purpose?*
- *What is your first emotional
  response to the story?*
- *In what ways do the pictures
  complement and interact with the
  text?*
- *What qualities may have appealed
  to the judges in making their
  selection for this award?*
- *Do you agree with the judges who
  said:*
  *In pared-back text and sombre
  colours, this powerful and moving
  picture book for mature readers
  captures a moment of simple
  heroism and compassion which
  triggers unexpected camaraderie
  in the midst of war. The poignant
  story combines the true incident of
  the famous Christmas truce, where
  German and Allied armies broke
  off hostilities to sing 'Silent night'
  across the snowy battlefield, with a
  fictional story of a compassionate
  young soldier rescuing a trapped*

*robin. A whole-world experience is
captured in a tiny incident. Careful
research and respect for soldiers of
both armies are evident in the spare
text, which uses the present tense
to intensify the immediacy and
dramatic tension of the incident,
and in the close details of uniforms
and the minutiae of trench warfare.*[9]

Other picture story books

Students will be encouraged to read as
many of the following as possible:

Rose Blanche by Roberto Innocenti,
Creative Editions, Minnesota, USA,
1984
*During Word War II, a young German
girl's curiosity leads her to discover
something far more terrible than
day-to-day hardships and privations
that she and her neighbours have
experienced. Excellent teaching
material available at
http://www.dramavictoria.vic.edu.au
/resources/lessons/perspective_of_
children_during_wartime.htm*

Let the Celebrations Begin by
Margaret Wilde and Julie Vivas,
Orchard Books, 1996
*This is a child's view of the release of
prisoners by the British at the end of
World War II.*

The Angel with the Mouth Organ by
Christabel Mattingley, illustrated by
Astra Lacis, Hodder and Stoughton
1984
*This is the story of a close-knit family's
flight from their homeland in a time
war, told from a child's point of view.*

Whole brain learning,
whole brain assessment:
Examplar units for
English and History

A Different Sort of Real: The Diary of Charlotte McKenzie, Melbourne 1918–19 by Kerry Greenwood, Ashton Scholastic, 2001. Shortlisted for the Children's Book Council Picture Story Book Award, 2002
13-year-old Charlotte recounts the year in which her soldier father and uncle return home; her father has shellshock and can't relate to the family, her uncle has been wounded but tries to tough it out.

My Hiroshima by Junko Morimoto, Angus and Robertson, 1988
The dropping of the first atomic bomb on the Japanese city of Hiroshima in 1945, told through the eyes of a child who was there at the time.

My Dog by John Heffernan and Andrew McLean, Margaret Hamilton Books, 2001
The story of a family forced to flee from their village during the recent Yugoslav civil war.

Memorial by Gary Crewe and Shaun Tan, Lothian, 1999
This book takes up the ideas of Anzac Day and war memorials and what they symbolise. Superb illustrations but a less satisfactory text.

Other print resources

Soldier Boy by Anthony Hill, Penguin, 2001
The true story of Jim Martin, the youngest Anzac.

All Quiet on the Western Front by Erich Maria Remarque, Pan Paperback, 1995
A novel from World War I, written from a German perspective.

Fly Away Peter by David Malouf, Vintage, 1998
A story set in the marshes of southern Queensland and the trenches of France in World War I.

I am David by Anne Holm, Harcourt Children's Books, 2004
The story of a boy trying to find his parents at the end of World War II.

When the Guns Fall Silent by James Riordan, Oxford University Press, 2000 – may currently be out of print
This novel includes poetry and snippets from songs at the start of each chapter and weaves in male, female, home front, Western Front and other perspectives.

Generals Die in Bed: A Story from the Trenches by Charles Yale Harrison, Penguin, 2002

Men who Marched Away
An anthology of poetry from World War I.

History texts and Web resources

Most secondary history text books have good information on World War I.
For example:

Australia and the Twentieth Century World, R. Darlington, J. Hospodaryk, and P. Cupper, Heinemann

A History of Australia Since 1901,
R. Darlington, and J. Hospodaryk,
Heinemann

**Investigating Australia's Twentieth
Century History**, Nelson (Thomson
Learning)

**Australia and the World in the
Twentieth Century**, Nelson History 3,
Nelson (Thomson Learning)

*There is an excellent web site with
pictures and information from our
National Library, The Australian War
Memorial, The National Archives,
Fryer Library of the University of
Queensland and the State Libraries of
Victoria, Tasmania and NSW.*

http://www.pictureaustralia.org/

*Here is the web site of all the
Australian museums.*

http://amol.org.au/discovernet/

*Use a search engine for a specific
topic or try
http://www.trenchesontheweb.com/*

Report writing activities

*Choose **one aspect of World War I** to
study such as:*
* *The life of Australian soldiers in the
  trenches*
* *Battle tactics and the nature of
  trench warfare*
* *The spontaneous Christmas
  armistice*
* *Annotation and recording of songs
  from World War I*
* *Examine propaganda from the
  time, especially the conscription
  propaganda in Australia*

* *Cartoons and propaganda posters
  from the time with an analysis of
  what they convey*
* *The life of Matahari or Nurse Carroll
  or Vivian Bullwinkle or Nancy
  Wake, or Sir John Monash, or other
  significant figures from the war*
* *Consequences for children and life
  at home during the war*
* *Or any other topic which the
  student finds of interest.*

Extension and thinking activities – ways of commemoration

*War memorials can reveal much about
a nation, the way it represents war,
national identity and what people
regard as important.*
* *Choose a local War Memorial.
  When was it built? Was the site
  significant? Which wars are
  remembered? How is the war
  remembered? How are the soldiers
  remembered? For example,
  are there statues, stained glass
  windows, poems, names? Are both
  men and women represented? What
  do you think the various elements
  of the war memorial symbolise
  to the nation? How can the public
  participate in commemoration? For
  example, what ceremonies take
  place? Has there been any debate
  about the war memorial? Why?
  When? What does this say about
  conflict and unity in that nation?*

Whole brain learning,
whole brain assessment:
Examplar units for
English and History

- *Make an analysis of the Australian War Memorial web site. Annotate a screen dump of the first one or two pages in order to read the meaning of the site and to examine the visual language. What images are on the Splash Page? What is the first list of contents? What does this indicate about how the site is used? What do you think are the purposes of the site? Is it to explain the War Memorial, for information, research, to explain commemorations?*
- *Make a comparison between an Australian War Memorial and one overseas. How are they different or similar? What does this say about the differences or similarities between how nations represent war?*
- *Compare Anzac Day with commemoration ceremonies or special days in other countries. Why do you think there has been a recent increase in commemorating wars with an increase in visits to Gallipoli, more attending Anzac Day marches and the building of the recent new shrine in London? Is this just 'glorification' of war or redefining the 'Australian spirit' in terms of war?*

Final task – prepare a narrative on World War I

*You will do this by preparing an electronic **picture story book in PowerPoint**.*

Your book will be aimed for an audience of middle Primary children.

It will contain:
- *a maximum of 12 slides;*
- *one picture per slide or a collage of pictures, if there are related ideas or images which you have drawn or scanned in;*
- *brief sentences on each page appropriate to the audience and complementary to the visual and aural material;*
- *some slides to contain, where appropriate, links to music, sound effects, video clips, cartoons, documents or other material which may enhance the reader's understanding of the story.*

Evaluate the picture story book according to the criteria you set out for yourself in the first activity.

What did we achieve?

As a response to the extension and thinking activities suggested above, one student decided to examine a war memorial in a park near his home more closely. In many ways the report is unexceptional but is significant in that the student chose the topic, followed up the information and was able to illustrate the report with some pictures he took with a digital camera borrowed from the school. This is just the first paragraph from the report:

> War memorials can be found all over Australia which are dedicated to different wars like the World Wars and the Vietnam War. They usually consist of some sort of a tribute to the deceased soldiers like a marble wall, a statue, a flag pole or a garden and they are there to remind us of the soldiers who fought and died for Australia and as an honour to their sacrifice.
>
> The war memorial that I chose to do some research on is one that stands in Halliday Park in Mitcham.

After class activities in the Flanders Fields unit above, which the teachers used in a variety of ways, each class at the year level nominated their best Picture Story Book. At a Year level assembly, the selected student from each class presented their story and the best was judged jointly by the Principal and

the Head of Creative Arts. It was a very worthwhile conclusion to the task and demonstrated a huge range of responses. Here are two slides by a student who drew his own pictures:

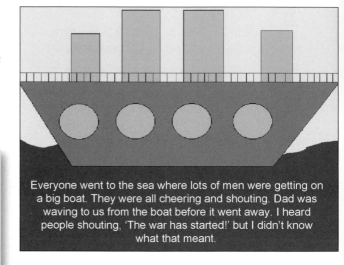

Everyone went to the sea where lots of men were getting on a big boat. They were all cheering and shouting. Dad was waving to us from the boat before it went away. I heard people shouting, 'The war has started!' but I didn't know what that meant.

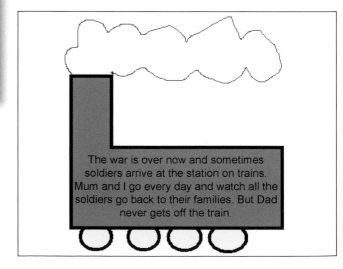

The war is over now and sometimes soldiers arrive at the station on trains. Mum and I go every day and watch all the soldiers go back to their families. But Dad never gets off the train.

**Whole brain learning,
whole brain assessment:
Examplar units for
English and History**

This student went about the task in quite a different way by importing pictures to illustrate a very unusual perspective on the First World War, but one that he has picked up from the *In Flanders Fields* starting point:

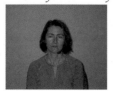

One German soldier thought about the Allies. He had seen some of them when they had made an earlier charge and they didn't seem very different from himself. They just happened to fight on the enemy side.

Image: Australian War memorial Negative Number E02306/

In the following response, the student has written from the perspective of a child left at home and he has illustrated the story with very simple imported pictures. Here are two slides from the story:

Annabelle observed from her chair, the changes around her. Her father taped the windows up, and her mother hoarded food in the cupboards.

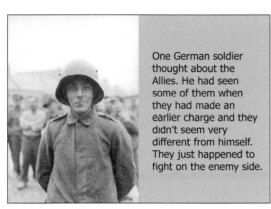

Annabelle saw her mother's face; it had changed. Gaunt and pale, the usual colourful cheery eyes were blank and expressionless.

When Annabelle woke up her mother had gone, the half-empty suitcase laid sprawled open on the dusty concrete floor. She walked to the door where the morning sunlight shone through in fingers. Her world had taken new shape.

A line of monsters crawled through the streets, and men holding guns were yelling and running. A truck full of people rolled slowly behind a monster and her mother was standing there yelling for Annabelle.

There are hundreds of ways the suggestions above could be followed up, depending on the interests of the class and the extent to which the teacher is prepared to take risks. The above units are merely examples of what may be possible. We trust that teachers will find some ideas to apply to their own texts or topics and to suit their own syllabus, class and teaching style.

Endnotes

1 D. Tapscott, *Growing up digital: the rise of the net generation*, McGraw Hill, NY, 1998.

2 B. Johnstone, *Never mind the laptops: kids, computers and the transformation of learning iUniverse*, Lincoln NE, 2003, p. 233.

3 'enGauge® 21st Century Skills: Literacy in the Digital Age 2003', The North Central Regional Educational Laboratory, viewed 7 June 2004, <http://www.ncrel.org/engauge/skills/skills.htm>

4 B. Johnstone, op.cit., 2003, p. 252.

5 J. Edwards, 'Learning and the teaching of thinking', IARTV, Seminar Series Paper, No. 88, October 1999.

6 This unit was developed in conjunction with Joe Carrozzi, librarian at Knox Grammar School, Sydney.

7 This unit was prepared by Year 9 History teachers at Carey Baptist Grammar School, Melbourne, under the guidance of the Head of Middle School Humanities, Sarah North, and the Director of E Learning, Elisabeth Lenders.

8 This multi-disciplinary task was devised together with Di McDonald, History teacher at Trinity Grammar School, Melbourne.

9 CBA Judges Report 2003, *Reading Time*, the journal of the Children's Book Council of Australia, Vol. 47, No. 3, August 2003.

Final reflections

Some experienced teachers will say, 'Leave it to the young ones coming out of teacher training; they will know what to do'. Strangely enough, it seems to be the older, experienced teachers who are often the most enthusiastic proponents of ICT. It is they who are confident in their discipline and have a well-tuned antenna as to what makes good learning and what engages students, so they are more ready to grasp the nettle and integrate online learning into their classrooms.[1]

This book has been designed to share examples of innovative practice with secondary Humanities teachers. The approach has been based on certain principles or assumptions which have been dealt with in various ways throughout the text. The following is by way of summary:

- Innovation does not happen in isolation. We don't need to rush for the overkill and change everything at once. Let us just take small risks, make incremental changes and do so in a team with the support of colleagues and critical friends.

- 'Knowledge, values and good thinking are … key ingredients in the educational process'.[2] Computers are a significant new tool to learn with and to think with, so let's not undervalue them as simply a safe, attractive word processing and presentation gizmo.

- Constructivist teachers value children as makers of meaning, creative learners and thinkers. Schneiderman, however, warns us that creativity is not universally valued. 'Many cultures and communities prefer training students to accept existing structures rather than training them to form new ones; they prefer memorisation and copying to research and creative writing.'[3] His book poses the intriguing question of how Leonardo da Vinci might have used a laptop and what applications he could have created.

- Teachers, not technicians, must be the driving force if there is to be any innovative change in teaching and learning as a result of the advent of computers. The inhibitors of change are not essentially hardware problems or money or the adequacy of software or the competence of technicians, but the reticence of teachers to change. It does not require heroic efforts but an admission of the need to learn in small steps and a culture in the school that supports risk-taking initiatives. Students will probably always have more skills than most teachers, but we cannot watch it all go by and remain fringe-dwellers in a rapidly developing but alien culture.

- If we are to introduce computers into our classrooms, a different classroom management model is required for this kind of learning to be successful. 'Teachers, in creating this environment, must become more of a "guide" and less of an "expert" which can be difficult for teachers who are used to being the provider of direct instruction all the time.'[4]

- Giving students laptops or equipping good labs is just the beginning. There is no point in having expensive, delicate hardware if there is no measurable impact on learning. Entrepreneur Bruce Dixon posed the challenge in the very early days of computer implementation: 'How do you get the teacher to decide that it's worthwhile taking the risk to change what they are doing, to implement technology to produce better outcomes for kids?'[5] His answer was that we

'identify successful models, show-case innovative practice and spread the good word', something he has been doing very actively for more than ten years with Australia-wide conferences.

- The computer will inevitably become a learning tool that is as invisible as a pen or pencil. Teachers just need to choose the right medium for the task and then focus on the task itself, not the medium. Laptops or personal computers become an individual workspace, and with adequate prior experience, the decision of a student to use Word or Excel or PowerPoint or paper or crayons will depend on the task and the way the student chooses to respond. We do not need to set a computer-based task for the sake of making use of the equipment. It is the learning that matters.

- Real learning is often measured by clear thinking, accurate expression, cohesive organisation and detailed understandings, not attractive presentations and neatly printed documents. Computers can be a great asset in this promotion of real learning. Let's not be sidetracked by computer gimmicks!

'Change is a journey, not a blue print', says Michael Fullan.[6] May this be both an encouragement and a useful guidebook on your journey.

Endnotes

[1] C. Murray, 'The crossroads: e-pedagogy and e-curriculum', *EQ Australia*, Melbourne, No. 4, Summer 2002, p. 21.

[2] L. Splitter & A. Sharp, *Teaching for better thinking*, ACER, Melbourne, 1995. p. 1.

[3] B. Schneiderman, *Leonardo's laptop: human needs and the new computing technologies*, MIT Press, Cambridge, Massachusetts, 2003, p. 131.

[4] D. McDonald, 'Hypertext and historical literacy', doctoral thesis under preparation for submission to Monash University, 2004.

[5] B. Johnstone, *Never mind the laptops: kids, computers and the transformation of learning iUniverse*, Lincoln NE, 2003, p. 329.

[6] M. Fullan, *Leading in a culture of change*, Jossey-Bass, San Francisco, 2001.

Appendix 1

Linking student tasks with curriculum objectives

Chapter	Subject or Key Learning Area	Task	Some links between tasks and curriculum objectives
3	All, especially Science, History	Concept mapping	Present information in different forms and for different purposes and audiences.
3	English, Art, Religious Instruction	Close reading of Shakespeare and other texts Study of sacred texts	Apply strategies to support understanding of complex or extended texts.
4	English, History, Geography, Science, Art, LOTE	Annotation of text Detailed reading of text	Use a variety of brief note-form responses to summarise or précis essential information and understandings. Read literature, daily print and media texts and construct interpretive responses supported by evidence.
4	English, History	Annotation of cartoons	Discuss and interpret the way a newsworthy event is presented in a variety of ways.
4	English, History	Newspaper opinion analysis	Demonstrate an understanding of the visual, auditory and written ways opinions are presented. Critically interpret a range of texts that present challenging themes and issues.

Chapter	Subject or Key Learning Area	Task	Some links between tasks and curriculum objectives
5, 6	All	Oral – formal and classroom discussion, group activities	Prepare and present oral performances. Use a range of strategies to influence an audience. Listen to, evaluate and produce a range of spoken texts dealing with challenging themes and issues.
6	English, History, Geography	Discussion of controversial contemporary issues and text responses	Ask relevant questions and respond constructively to new ideas and information.
7	English	Informative and instructional writing	Write a variety of texts, including web pages, hyperlinked documents or newspaper articles, which explain, argue, persuade or report. Adjust writing for a range of contexts, purposes and audiences. Use a range of strategies to plan, compose, revise and edit texts.
7	English, Art	Close study of Shakespeare	Apply a variety of strategies to support understanding of complex or extended texts. Use hyperlinks to explore understanding.
7	Geography	Fact sheet and analysis	Use hyperlinks to present research.
8	English	Visual response to poetry	Generate and expressively develop ideas when making and presenting visual communication.
8	History, Geography	Research and analysis of contemporary issues	Construct a timeline of significant events. Select resources to support a point or view on a contemporary issue.
9	All	Selection, analysis and annotation of web resources	Select, collate, annotate and synthesise meaningful and reliable resources and data. Organise resources for future reference.
9	English	Argumentative writing	Identify, explain and use techniques to influence an audience.

Chapter	Subject or Key Learning Area	Task	Some links between tasks and curriculum objectives
11	History, English	Research of historical events and accompanying literature	Research and present significant events and ideas in a variety of modes, such as concept maps, verbal recorded reports, oral presentations, annotation of text, creative responses combining music, art and other modes of response.
11	All subjects	Open ended assessment tasks	Use a range of assessment strategies to encourage student choice and allow for a range of thinking styles.

Curriculum reviews are currently being undertaken around the country. One example comes from the Victorian Curriculum and Assessment Authority which published a discussion paper in 2004 as part of their Curriculum Reform Project. In their Guide to the Proposed Reform of Victorian Curriculum,[1] they listed, among other things, some challenges which are particularly pertinent to the theme of this book. They argue for a curriculum which will:

- enable students to develop the skills and attributes expected of people in a modern society;
- encourage students to think their way through issues and problems;
- promote innovation and variety in teaching, according to the needs of students and the communities in which they live;
- promote a range of assessment procedures.

In their research for this project, they identified the desire in schools for, among others things:

- the ability to use innovative and flexible teaching styles to achieve the best learning outcomes for students;
- more focus on depth of understanding rather than breadth of content;
- the provision of skills, values and attributes that promote life-long learning.

Essential cross-curriculum skills include:

- communication skills (reading, writing listening speaking, information and communication technology, drawing, performance) and thinking skills (e.g. inquiring reasoning, problem solving, evaluation).

In the summary of the proposed changes, one significant point is:

- … the new approach will explicitly recognise the importance of values and the ability of students to apply what they have learnt to new situations through deep understanding.

Endnotes

[1] See <http://www.vcaa.vic.edu.au/prep10/crp/consultGuide.pdf>, viewed 1/02/05.

Appendix 2

Software packages

The author has used a number of software packages in the classroom to supplement and extend the student activities. He recommends these products but gains no financial advantage from doing so.

1 Inspiration

Examples using Inspiration software can be found on pages 20, 22, 23, 24, 25 and 26.

If Inspiration is new to you and you have downloaded a free one-month trial version of the software[1], here are some suggestions:

1 Find your way around the program by using it: In the first Main Idea, type the phrase, 'Terrorism curbs overseas travel' OR 'Year 12 students at this school are spoon fed and lack initiative' OR 'The "Stolen Generation" is a myth perpetuated by the black arm band view of our history'.

2 Now create four other circles, two with reasons for and two against.

3 Put in links between the central box and the four others. Try putting in a link between the outer boxes. The most useful part of this program for students is the requirement that they name the links, as this forces them to think through the relationships.

4 Now put a few sentences of notes behind the boxes.

5 Experiment with the icons and the colours. Change the background of the screen and of each box or change each box into a symbol after browsing the symbol palette. Look at the Outline View, Notes View, Zoom in, Zoom out function, change the position of the boxes, select text from any Word Document on your computer and Paste it into one of the Notes boxes. Do the same with a picture from clip art or the Web. Just play to familiarise yourself with the program.

6 Have a look at the templates (File/Templates) set up for each subject. They are a good starting point, although generally students prefer to create their own maps.

7 Now start another new Inspiration document. This time, put in as the Main Idea a concept from one of your texts or topics, or some other open-ended 'thinking question' such as:
- Juliet's foolishness led to tragedy in the play *Romeo and Juliet* OR
- Hamlet hid behind excuses OR
- *The Lord of the Rings* is a boring movie OR
- Our team is performing badly because of poor leadership OR
- Medicare is not economically viable in its current form OR
- Arab slave trading in Africa was the 'jihad' of the eighteenth century OR
- Australia's water resources are badly managed
- Use Inspiration as a flow chart to detail the process of getting a crop or livestock from farm to consumer
- any other open-ended and provocative topic.

2 SchoolKiT

An excellent commercial resource is SchoolKiT, which is accessed online, enabling the teacher to browse, select and download hundreds of learning modules across the Arts, Mathematics, Science, Social Studies, English and cross-curricular activities. Modules are organised under subjects and year levels.

Examples using SchoolKiT software can be found on pages 89, 107 and 119.

For further details, see the web site at http://www.schoolkit.com and click on EDclass OR go directly to the EDclass web site http://www.edclass.com

3 ProBoards

ProBoards is free and easy-to-use, though not password protected and contains minimal advertising, generally of tourist destinations. It is useful for setting up a discussion group in the classroom. Examples using Proboards software can be found on page 75.

The web site address is http://www.proboards.com/index.html

4 Hot Potatoes

Hot Potatoes (referred to in chapter 10) is a suite of six applications enabling users to create interactive multiple choice, short-answer, jumbled-sentence, crossword, matching/ordering and gap-fill exercises for the World Wide Web. Hot Potatoes is not freeware, but it is free of charge for those working for publicly-funded, non-profit-making educational institutions, who make their pages available on the Web. Other users must pay for a licence. Check out the Hot Potatoes licensing terms and prices on the Half-Baked software web site at http://web.uvic.ca/hrd/halfbaked.

Endnotes

1 See <http://www.inspiration.com>.

Index

WITHDRAWN

MAY 0 7 2024

DAVID O. McKAY LIBRARY
BYU-IDAHO